# Greenmarket

# Greenmarket

## THE COMPLETE GUIDE TO
## NEW YORK CITY'S FARMERS MARKETS

### WITH 55 RECIPES

BY Pamela Thomas

PHOTOGRAPHS BY Andrea Sperling

FOREWORD BY BARRY BENEPE, FOUNDER OF GREENMARKET

STEWART, TABORI & CHANG
*New York*

JACKET AND BOOK DESIGN BY
*BTDnyc*

Text copyright © 1999 Pamela Thomas

Photographs copyright © 1999 Andrea Sperling

Illustrations on pp. 33 and 34-37 copyright © 1999 Neil Packer

Additional copyrighted acknowledgments can be found on page 254

Published in 1999 by
Stewart, Tabori & Chang
A division of U.S. Media Holdings, Inc.
115 West 18th Street
New York, NY 10011

Distributed in Canada by
General Publishing Company Ltd.
30 Lesmill Road
Don Mills, Ontario, Canada M3B 2T6

LIBRARY OF CONGRESS CATALOGING-IN-PUBLICATION DATA

Thomas, Pamela, 1946-
   Greenmarket : the complete guide to New York City's farmers markets / by Pamela Thomas ; photographs by Andrea Sperling.

p. cm.

Includes index.

—ISBN 1-55670-916-1

1. Farm produce—New York (State)—New York—Marketing—Guidebooks. 2. Farmers' markets—New York (State)—New York—Guidebooks.

I. Title.
HD9008.N5T48          1999
641.5—dc21            99-19192
                                              CIP

Printed in Italy by Mondadori

10 9 8 7 6 5 4 3 2 1

# Contents

*Encyclopedia of
Greenmarket Produce*

# *Farmer Portraits*

# Foreword

BY BARRY BENEPE, FOUNDER OF GREENMARKET

In late 1975, my colleague, Bob Lewis, and I were discussing what could be done to stop the loss of farmland in our region. As professional planners, we frequently advised regional communities on how to keep suburban sprawl from ruining their beautiful towns and countryside. Still, we saw clearly that existing environmental programs were unable to stem the loss of regional farmland.

New York City consumers were also getting a raw deal. Fresh produce was often unavailable in city supermarkets, while fresh vegetables and fruits were dying on the trees because farmers had no outlet.

If farmers were to remain part of our regional fabric, they had to be able to market their produce profitably. The central question seemed to be: How can farmers earn a decent living off their land? Bob's and my solution was to try to set up a market in New York City where farmers could sell directly to consumers.

At that time, my father reminded me of my boyhood experience on our truck farm on the Eastern Shore of Maryland. We grew tomatoes, cucumbers, string beans, and Fordhook lima beans that we sold at local markets. Ours was a "gentleman's farm," since my father earned his living in New York City. Still, my father was determined that the farm pay for itself, and because of this, I experienced firsthand the marketing problems faced by farmers.

For example, wholesale buyers could rig prices by agreeing not to bid against each other. To get around this, my brother, Bruce, would sometimes drive to New York City, an eight-hour trip, with 300 bushels of beans just to get an additional 50 cents a bushel. This almost-forgotten lesson strengthened my resolve to find an effective method for farmers to sell profitably.

In the mid-1970s, Bob and I were not the only people interested in farmers markets. Writer John Hess spoke glowingly of a

*Barry Benepe at Union Square, Fall 1998*

market in Syracuse, and lamented the loss of Manhattan's historic Washington Market. Elinor Guggenheimer, then New York's Commissioner of Consumer Affairs, publicly proclaimed the desirability of farmers markets for consumers. Fortunately, within months of Bob's and my decision to create a market, the Council on the Environment of New York City enthusiastically adopted the Greenmarket program. (Marian Heiskell, then chairperson and now honorary chairperson of the Council, has been especially helpful from the start.)

Slowly our goals coalesced and our management techniques were refined. For example, after a grower from Long Island arrived one day with bananas to sell, we tightened our regulations, insisting that farmers could sell only what they grew. By eliminating middlemen, we insured that farmers reaped a reasonable profit while consumers enjoyed a tremendous variety of fresh produce—often at a savings over supermarket prices.

Today, Greenmarket has been running successfully for 23 years. Several years ago, Bob Lewis moved on to a state post, but I stayed, stepping down as director in 1998, but remaining as a consultant.

For years I have wanted a book that would serve as a guide to Greenmarket, and here it is. Pamela Thomas is the ideal author, having demonstrated in her series *From Garden to Table* her knowledge of the relationship between growing food and eating it. For this book Pam has also highlighted the special bond that exists between the farmers and New York consumers, a link that forms the heart of Greenmarket. This book will introduce you to new ideas about food, farmers, and our environment. Use it with pleasure.

# Relishing Abundance
## Notes from the Author

I have the good fortune to live only a five minute walk from the flagship Union Square Greenmarket. Over the many months that I worked on this book, I explored the market religiously. During virtually every excursion, I would come across some new item—an exotic herb, an obscure berry, a miniature hot pepper—that not only had I not yet profiled in the book, but had never seen before. I would return to my desk utterly overwhelmed. There was *just too much*!

After enduring this frustrating exercise repeatedly—and sensing that I could never stay on top of it—I finally decided to sit back, relax (sort of), and simply relish the abundance of Greenmarket. And I urge readers to do the same.

### Abundance: A Guide

Growers bring more than 1,000 varieties of vegetables, fruits, greens, herbs, and other products to Greenmarket. This book will serve as a general shopping guide to this produce. As a consumer, you can tuck the book in your backpack or purse, then turn to it for information and ideas as you peruse the markets. If you come across some variety that is not included in the book, just ask the farmer to fill you in about it.

To help you locate particular markets, a current "New York City Greenmarket Locations" map has been designed (page 33) detailing the directions to all 27 Greenmarkets in the metropolitan area. To alert you to seasonal specialties, a "Greenmarket Harvest Calendar" (pages 34 to 37) has also been created. The calendar is supported by a design element that appears near the bottom of the page in each entry. The element consists of four circles indicating the seasons. If the circle is colored, the product is available (even if it is only available dried or cold-storaged). For example, potatoes are available year-round, so all four seasons are colored:

W   S   S   F

## THE ENCYCLOPEDIA

The heart of this book is an "Encyclopedia of Greenmarket Produce" with entries for over 200 varieties of vegetables, fruits, and other products regularly sold at Greenmarket. Within each entry, I have provided notes on selection, storage, preservation, and preparation.

Preserving food can present special problems. Depending on the type of food and the length of time it is meant to be stored, preserving can be accomplished by canning, freezing, drying, cold storage, smoking, and pickling. Some of these processes can be complicated, even dangerous, if not done correctly. Consult a good preserving guide for instructions.

## THE RECIPES

I have included a recipe or preparation instruction for almost every entry in the book. Some of the recipes are my own, others come from Greenmarket farmers, and still others come from some of the chefs and food writers who have long been devoted to Greenmarket, including Michael Romano, Mario Batali, Martha Stewart, Larry Forgione, and Jean-Georges Vongerichten. Except in cases where I could not resist something I found incredibly delicious, I have tried to select recipes that are relatively easy. This is especially true for those foods that can sometimes seem a bit intimidating to prepare or eat, like kohlrabi or celeriac.

## THE FARMERS

Over 200 growers participate in Green-market, many of whom have been part of the program for years. Of course, I wanted to interview all of them, but the same "just too much" frustration entered into these plans as well. As it turns out, I have included 22 portraits of Greenmarket growers and purveyors, 13 of whom I was able to visit at their farms.

As far as I was concerned, exploring regional farms was the best part of creating this book. I was struck by the gorgeous countryside that surrounds New York City, and by the generosity and graciousness of the growers.

But most especially, I was deeply impressed with how hard these farmers worked. By participating in Greenmarket, most growers work two full-time jobs. First, they manage their farms. Then, several days each week, they arise at 3 A.M., drive for two or three hours into New York City, work for ten hours selling their produce, then pack up and drive another three hours home. Still, each farmer confirmed how much he appreciated the existence of Greenmarket and cherished his relationships with New York customers.

## THE PHOTOGRAPHS

While I was working on this book, I heard about Andrea Sperling, a professional photographer who, over a period of several years, had taken scores of black-and-white portraits of Greenmarket produce. Andrea's pictures were beautiful works of art, and I loved them. Nevertheless, for this book, we needed straightforward shots of fruits and vegetables together with action photos of the colorful and abundant life at the markets.

Andrea turned to her job with great aplomb, and thankfully, her terrific artist's eye remained in evidence. Of course, the infernal "just too much" issue arose again, and Andrea produced an embarrassment of photographic riches. We relished it all, then used what we we able to fit into a book of economic length.

## THE GREENMARKET STORY

Finally, this little book is actually two books in one: A shopper's guide as well as a short history of this vital entity called Greenmarket. I hope you will take the time to savor the extended introduction, "Greenmarket: Its Life & Times." It's a marvelous and important story.

# Greenmarket: Its Life & Times

O n any given day of the week, during every week of the year, as you walk around the city of New York, you may come upon an open space lined with white canopied booths. You may suspect that you've lucked upon a festive street fair replete with Charlie Parker wannabes, Jack Russell terriers sporting miniature Yankee baseball caps, babies in strollers, grandpas with walkers, society matrons draped in downtown black, and drag queens decked out in sequined pink.

No, this is not a set from a Fellini film. It's a farmers market, and as you take a closer look, you'll see the best part of all: an incredible array of fresh produce. In stand after stand, you'll find vegetables, fruits, cut flowers, and potted plants alongside sumptuous arrangements of meats, fish, cheeses, jams, honey, and even lamb's wool yarn in blissful colors. If it's spring, you'll be intoxicated with the aroma of lilacs; if it's summer, you'll be bowled over with the scent of fresh strawberries (June) or peaches (August); if it's fall, you'll be dazzled with the sight of bright orange pumpkins piled high. Even in winter, you'll be impressed with the abundance of foods held in cold storage for urban consumers, including cabbages, turnips, parsnips, apples,

*Above and opposite: The Union Square Greenmarket*

*Washington Market Park, Tribeca*

in school yards, parking lots, and on street corners. They vary in size from the large market at Union Square which boasts as many as 80 stands during the summer, to the tiny market that operates year-round on Sundays near Tompkins Square.

Greenmarket is one of several programs that make up the Council on the Environment of New York City, a privately funded citizens' organization in the office of New York's mayor. Begun in 1970, the Council on the Environment promotes environmental awareness among New Yorkers. (Its other activities include creating urban gardens, educating school children about the environment, designing waste prevention systems for businesses, and promoting noise abatement.)

To sell at Greenmarket, more than 200 farmers and food producers come from generally a 100-mile median-radius of Manhattan—including upstate New York, New Jersey, Pennsylvania, Connecticut, and Long Island. Some farmers come from as far as 300 miles away, and many come as often as three or four days per week. Currently, a Greenmarket is in operation somewhere in the city every day of the week, every week of the year. Its purpose is to sup-

and potatoes. At Christmas time, there's no better place to find a tree, garlands of evergreens, and scores of special presents.

This is a New York City Greenmarket, one of 33 farmers markets that operate in 27 locations dotted around the city. (The numbers vary because several sites operate more than one day per week.) Markets are found

port farmers, preserve farmland, and ensure a continuing supply of fresh local produce to consumers. This is accomplished by providing an opportunity for regional growers to sell their products directly to New Yorkers.

## THE PLIGHT OF REGIONAL FARMERS

The land surrounding New York City is incredibly rich. When driving past the strip malls that pepper the northern Bronx or the smelly manufacturing plants that line the highways in nearby New Jersey, it is almost impossible to fathom that these urban blights are built on farmland that was once considered some of the choicest on the planet. Lest we forget, the nickname for New Jersey is the "Garden State"! Perhaps less well known but equally lush is the "Black Dirt" region around Warwick, New York, that has long been known to agrarians as an absolute Shangri-la for vegetable growers.

*Right: The lush "Black Dirt" of Orange County, New York*

Until after World War II, a lively business relationship existed between regional growers whose farms thrived less than an hour's drive from the city and urban consumers who nearly took for granted the delectable vegetables available to them, such as vine-ripened tomatoes from New Jersey and freshly picked sweet corn from upper Westchester. Over the past 50 years, however, close to a million acres of farmland in this region have been lost to what might be described as "creeping suburbia."

After World War II, GIs and their families welcomed the affordable housing provided by developers like William Levitt, the easy-access highways created by public officials like Robert Moses, and the increasingly ubiquitous shopping centers put up by God knows who. What people failed to notice was that these suburban delights were eating up farmland.

*Poe Park Greenmarket, The Bronx*

To complicate matters, and as a result of scientific and technological advancements, large-scale industrial growers began to make profound inroads into the New York urban market. Agribusiness farmers, especially those from the Southwest, Mexico, and the West Coast, bred produce for looks as well as for the ability to be transported economically. Tomatoes, peaches, plums, and apples, among many other fruits and vegetables, could be shipped into New York City bruise free, look great on a supermarket shelf, and last longer than most homegrown varieties.

In addition, consumers were growing more and more addicted to processed foods, from TV dinners to take-out burgers and fries, finger-lickin' chicken, and ersatz Italian pizzas. The major corporations that produced the fast food turned to big agribusiness farmers for the vast supplies of chicken, beef, milk, potatoes, onions, tomatoes, and other produce they needed. The fact that freshness and flavor had been sacrificed seemed not to matter—at least for a little while.

Small farmers were hit hard by these so-called advancements, and a vicious cycle developed. The city was growing in every direction, eating up the farmland; land taxes increased; the costs of wholesalers, retailers and other middlemen rose dramatically while competition from large growers caused prices paid for regional produce to drop. The small farmers became almost desperate. If a developer came along who wanted to buy land to build a shopping mall or a housing project, many small growers had no alternative but to sell to him. Which caused the city to sprawl. And on it went.

Farmers were not the only losers. Consumers paid twice for these developments. First, they lost quality in their food, in terms of freshness, nutrition, and flavor. Second, they lost the incredibly beautiful countryside that had once been so blessedly close to the city.

By the early 1970s, the farmers within one hour's drive of New York City had become all but extinct, the growers within two hours' drive were dying, and only a handful of environmentalists and a few back-to-the-earth hippies seemed to care.

Enter Barry Benepe.

## THE CONCEPTION OF GREENMARKET

In the early 1970s, Barry Benepe was working as an architect and city planner and raising his family in New York City. Having grown up on a farm in Maryland on the fertile Delmarva peninsula, Barry was familiar with farming and the problems sur-

*Grand Army Plaza Greenmarket, Brooklyn*

rounding selling produce at market. Not surprisingly, he was also an avid environmentalist. In particular, he was concerned that agribusiness was robbing humanity of fresh, locally grown food.

This situation came into stark relief one autumn day in 1974 when he began chatting with a fruit broker at a farm belonging to a developer in Orange County who was considering building a housing project on the land. Benepe assumed that the fruit

broker would be disturbed by the loss of this farm's apples to his business, but instead the broker shrugged and said he assumed we would be buying all our apples from China within the decade.

The broker's attitude cut Barry to the quick. We wouldn't starve, he believed, but soon we would not be able to find a fruit or vegetable that had any honest flavor. Barry began talking to Hudson Valley farmers and quickly understood the fears of regional growers, many of whom were working land that had been in their families for several generations. He saw that these farmers, who usually worked less than 300 acres, could not compete with the giant agribusiness growers, but might be helped by selling directly to New York City consumers.

*St. Mark's Greenmarket, Manhattan*

Working with Barry in his New York office at this time was another environmentalist, Bob Lewis. (Today, Bob is director of marketing for the Department of Agriculture and Markets for New York State.) Barry and Bob had read about the success of a farmers market in Syracuse, New York, and began kicking around ideas for a farmers market in New York City along the same lines.

For two years, the notion existed only as an idea. Finally, early in 1976, Barry submitted a proposal for financial support to a number of private foundations who had expressed interest in the idea. Several responded positively and agreed to help. Barry and Bob were also encouraged by Elinor Guggenheimer, then the Commissioner for Consumer Affairs for New York City, who suggested that they approach the Council on the Environment of New York City as a sponsor.

The choice of the Council on the Environment proved to be an asset for Greenmarket; sort of the best of two worlds. Since the council was part of the office of the mayor, it permitted Greenmarket to have a helpful connection to the city, yet remain part of a privately funded organization.

Lys McLaughlin was the associate director of the council in 1975 when Barry and Bob first came into her office. (Lys became director in 1978, and remains in that position today.) As Lys puts it, "Barry showed up with a proposal to do a feasibility study. We suggested that it might be better just to start a market instead of simply studying it." So, the original study quickly evolved into a $36,000 program for a weekly farmers market in Manhattan, scheduled to open in the summer of 1976.

Suzanne Davis of the J.M. Kaplan Fund, one of the principal funders, suggested a city-owned parking lot at 59th Street and Second Avenue on the East Side of Manhattan as the site for the first market. Although the lot was relatively small, it was ideally situated between a high-income residential community (Manhattan's posh Sutton Place) and a busy shopping district that included Bloomingdale's department store.

Because the lot was used by the New York Police Department, intensive negotiations were necessary to secure permission for its use in time to sell produce harvested in late July. But Barry and Bob persisted. After careful presentation of the market's purpose to several boards and organizations and with enormous assistance from many public offices, Greenmarket was granted clearance.

Securing the space was just the first step. Now Barry and Bob had to convince farmers to come into Manhattan to sell. Bob personally called on individual farmers to explain the guidelines and selling practices. Still, nobody was certain if any of the growers would show up. Most were wary of New York City, fearing that they would be ripped off.

*Salad days: Bob Lewis (second from left), Lys McLaughlin, Barry Benepe with Barry's sons Callum, Andrew, and Simon, circa 1978.*

At 7 A.M. on July 17, 1976, seven growers from Long Island, New Jersey, and upstate New York arrived at the 59th Street site in pickup trucks and vans loaded with fresh-picked produce. As they began to arrange their stands, the farmers noticed a small but eager-looking crowd beginning to form outside the fence. Promptly at 8 A.M., the gates swung open.

Because it was the height of summer, the stands were piled high with vine-ripened tomatoes, crisp lettuce, raspberries, blueberries, and baby peaches. Best of all, the farmers came with truckloads of just-picked sweet corn. Unfortunately, the New Yorkers, used to shopping sales at Loehmann's or Macy's, were not on their best behavior. In a famous article entitled "Giving Good Weight," published several months later in *The New Yorker,* John McPhee described one farmer's impressions on that first day:

"The people were fifteen deep. I couldn't believe it. There were just masses of faces. I looked at them and felt panic and broke into a cold sweat. They went after the corn so fast I just dumped it on the ground. The people fell on it, stripped it, threw the husks around. They were fighting, grabbing, snatching at anything they could get their hands on. I had never seen anything like it. We sold a full truck in five hours. It was as if there was a famine going on."

By noon, all the farmers were sold out. And despite the bewildering behavior of the natives—or perhaps because of it—everyone considered Greenmarket a smashing success.

Two more markets opened that first summer. The second, on August 30, was located at Union Square, then a down-at-the-heels den of drug addicts. Barry and others worried about the location, not only because it was dangerous, but also because it was near neither a strong business center nor a thriving residential neighborhood. Still, the physical space was perfect for parking a dozen trucks. As it has turned out, Union Square has become synonymous with Greenmarket, and, in turn, Greenmarket has played a significant role in the revitalization of the entire Union Square district. A third market, located in central Brooklyn near the Academy of Music, also opened in late summer 1976.

Each year since, more markets have opened. Some have worked; some haven't. Nevertheless, by 1998, markets in 27 locations were thriving. (Other farmers markets that are not part of the Greenmarket program are also in operation; look for a Greenmarket logo.) Greenmarkets are located in every borough of the city, from Verdi Square in Manhattan, to Poe Park in The Bronx, McCarren Park in Brooklyn, Jackson Heights in Queens, and St. George Square on Staten Island.

## HOW DOES GREENMARKET OPERATE?

Unlike other famous markets, such as those in Philadelphia, Cleveland, and San Francisco, the hallmark of the Greenmarket is that participating farmers are permitted to sell only what they grow or produce (with a few exceptions). In addition to fruit

*Opposite: The first Greenmarket on 59th Street, July 1976*

*Barry Benepe with New York City Parks Commissioner Henry Stern at Greenmarket's 10th Anniversary celebration*

and vegetables, also sold are fish, meat, poultry, game, eggs, dairy products, maple syrup, honey, flowers, and plants. Only the regional growers, their family members, or employees may sell the produce at the market; no middlemen are allowed.

To insure that these principles are followed, Greenmarket managers and farmers developed a comprehensive set of rules and regulations. Selling only what you grow seems straightforward, but in certain instances it can prove complicated. For example, jams must be made by the purveyor, but he or she need not have grown all of the fruit contained in the preserves. In other words, an apple farmer can sell an apple-and-pear conserve made with pears grown on a neighbor's farm. Processes like pressing cider or spinning wool can be performed off-farm, so long as the end product contains a particular percentage of the grower's produce.

The matter of organic versus inorganic farming is another thorny issue. Greenmarket promotes all agriculture, not only organic farming; therefore some farmers use pesticides and some don't. However, if a farmer wants to advertise his produce as "organic," he must be certified by the appropriate associations.

Greenmarket is managed by the Greenmarket director, the assistant director, and a few administrative assistants. A manager is also on hand at each of the markets. Staff members or specially trained inspectors visit farms to make sure that what is sold on a grower's stand at the market is actually cultivated in his fields. Cider mills, dairy plants, bakeries, and other relevant establishments are also inspected to insure the integrity of the products sold at the market.

Dealing with the problems of more than 200 farmers requires knowledge and patience. To help Greenmarket administrators, the Farmer Consumer Advisory Committee (FCAC) was formed to advise on market problems and general policy. The committee is composed of fifteen Greenmarket growers and six consumers, including interested neighbors, local business people, and restaurateurs. The FCAC provides peer review when problems arise, and is used to secure input from growers on creating guidelines for various products.

Like any organization, Greenmarket needs money to function. The farmers pay a fee to the Council on the Environment to permit them to sell at the markets. Grants and contributions from many organizations and funds supplement the fees. For example, the Vinmont Foundation and the J.M. Kaplan Fund are just two of the foundations that have generously supported Greenmarket over the years.

## A GIFT TO NEW YORKERS

Greenmarket was conceived to help regional farmers, but it has proven to be an equally great gift to New Yorkers. A strong symbiotic relationship has evolved between Greenmarket farmers and their New York customers. For example, farmers bring in relatively unusual products, like baby kale or Yukon Gold potatoes, and consumers will buy them up readily—or not. In turn,

customers may inquire about rare varieties of greens, potatoes, or whatever, and the farmers will try growing an acre or two to see how it flourishes in the field and if it will sell at Greenmarket.

Growers who registered fear about coming into the city or bewilderment at the aggressiveness of their customers have flipped 180 degrees. They love New York and New Yorkers—and they are adored in return. This mutual affection is another layer in the bedrock of Greenmarket. The farmers appreciate the importance of the city as

*Farmland in New York's Hudson Valley*

*A sign for Greenmarket at the Staten Island ferry*

a marketplace, and city-bound residents view visiting Greenmarket almost like a trip to the country. Even children are enamored of the market. Not a week goes by that schoolchildren are not seen at one market or another, and often farmers bring lambs, calves, goats, or pigs to market to give kids a chance to learn about "exotic" farm animals.

Thanks to Greenmarket, not only has the average New York shopper become more discriminating about food, but professionals have become avid supporters as well. Many of New York's most acclaimed restaurateurs and chefs—Danny Meyer of Union Square Cafe, Peter Hoffman of Savoy (who serves on the FCAC), Jean-Georges Vongerichten of Vong, Larry Forgione of An American Place, Mario Batali of Babbo, just to name a few—credit Greenmarket with supplying their restaurants with the freshest ingredients and stimulating their creative juices on countless occasions. Other "foodies" like Martha Stewart have featured Greenmarket many times in their publications.

Greenmarket also participates in the New York State Farmers Market Nutrition Program, which every year distributes over $1 million worth of coupons that can be redeemed at Greenmarket for fresh produce. This program ensures that mothers who may be nutritionally at risk and their children will be well-fed, and that markets in lower-income neighborhoods can thrive.

## TODAY & TOMORROW

Today, more than 200 farmers (representing over 16,000 acres of cultivated land) participate in Greenmarket. Most of them would find it difficult if not impossible to stay in business without Greenmarket. What's more, many have been able to branch out creatively, growing foods that would not be viable to cultivate without the presence of the strong New York market.

In 1998, Barry Benepe retired as director of Greenmarket after 22 years. Tony Mannetta, formerly the assistant director, took over as director in July 1998. Joel Patraker, with the market since 1983, became the new assistant director.

Tony is eager to reach out to more communities while retaining Greenmarket's standards, uniqueness, and integrity. Under Tony's direction, several new neighborhood markets have already been established, including four in Brooklyn and one (located in the parking lot of a Korean market) in Queens.

*Greenmarket director Tony Mannetta*

For more than 20 years, Greenmarket has had a beneficial effect on the life of New York City. It serves as a reminder of the changing of the seasons and the importance of the earth. When asked if he was proud of being part of Greenmarket's creation, Bob Lewis said it was "mythical at some level."

Surely, Bob's observation is true. And surely, too, Greenmarket will grow, prosper, and bring joy and good food to New Yorkers for many years to come.

**MANHATTAN**

**1. BOWLING GREEN**
Broadway & Battery Park Place
*Thursday; year-round* • *8 AM – 5 PM*

**2. WORLD TRADE CENTER**
Church & Fulton Streets
*Tuesday; June to December*
*Thursday; year-round* • *8 AM – 5 PM*

**3. CITY HALL** • Chambers & Centre Streets
*Tuesday and Friday; year-round* • *8 AM – 3 PM*

**4. WASHINGTON MARKET PARK**
Greenwich & Chambers Streets
*Wednesday; year-round* • *8 AM – 3 PM*
**P.S. 234** • Greenwich & Chambers Streets
*Saturday; year-round* • *8 AM – 3 PM*

**5. FEDERAL PLAZA** • Broadway & Thomas Street
*Friday; year-round* • *8 AM – 4 PM*

**6. SOHO SQUARE** • Spring Street & Sixth Avenue
*Thursday; July to October* • *8 AM – 5 PM*

**7. TOMPKINS SQUARE**
East 7th Street & Avenue A
*Sunday; year-round* • *10 AM – 5 PM*

**8. ST. MARK'S CHURCH**
East 10th Street & Second Avenue
*Tuesday; June to December* • *8 AM – 7 PM*

**9. ABINGDON SQUARE**
West 12th Street & Eighth Avenue
*Saturday; May to December* • *8 AM – 1 PM*

**10. UNION SQUARE**
East 17th Street & Broadway
*Mon., Wed., Fri., Sat.; year-round* • *8 AM – 6 PM*

**11. SHEFFIELD PLAZA**
West 57th Street & Ninth Avenue
*Wednesday and Saturday; year-round* • *8 AM – 3 PM*

**12. VERDI SQUARE** • West 72nd Street & Broadway
*Saturday; June to December* • *8 AM – 5 PM*

**13. I.S. 44** • West 77th Street & Columbus Ave.
*Sunday; year-round* • *10 AM – 5 PM*

**14. 97TH STREET**
Between Amsterdam & Columbus Avenues
*Friday; June to December* • *8 AM – 2 PM*

**15. HARLEM** • West 144th Street & Lenox Avenue
*Tuesday; July to October* • *8 AM – 3 PM*

**16. 175TH STREET** • West 175th Street & Broadway
*Thursday; July to December* • *8 AM – 6 PM*

**BRONX**

**17. LINCOLN HOSPITAL** • 149th Street & Park Ave.
*Tuesday and Friday; July to October* • *8 AM – 3 PM*

**18. POE PARK** • Grand Concourse & 192nd Street
*Tuesday; July to October* • *8 AM – 2 PM*

**QUEENS**

**19. JACKSON HEIGHTS**
Junction Food Bazaar parking lot
Junction Boulevard & 34th Avenue
*Wednesday; July to October* • *8 AM – 3 PM*

**BROOKLYN**

**20. BOROUGH HALL** • Court & Remsen Streets
*Tuesday and Saturday; year-round* • *8 AM – 6 PM*

**21. ALBEE SQUARE**
Fulton Street & DeKalb Avenue
*Wednesday; July to October* • *8 AM – 3 PM*

**22. GRAND ARMY PLAZA**
Entrance to Prospect Park
*Saturday; year-round* • *8 AM – 4 PM*

**23. WINDSOR TERRACE**
Prospect Park West & 15th Street,
inside park entrance
*Wednesday; May to November* • *8 AM – 4 PM*

**24. BEDFORD-STUYVESANT**
Nostrand & DeKalb Avenues
*Saturday; July to October* • *8 AM – 3 PM*

**25. WILLIAMSBURG**
Havemeyer Street & Broadway
*Thursday; July to October* • *8 AM – 5 PM*

**26. McCARREN PARK**
Lorimer & Driggs Avenues
*Saturday; June to November* • *8 AM – 3 PM*

**STATEN ISLAND**

**27. ST. GEORGE** • Borough Hall
St. Mark's & Hyatt Streets (parking lot)
*Saturday; June to November* • *8 AM – 2 PM*

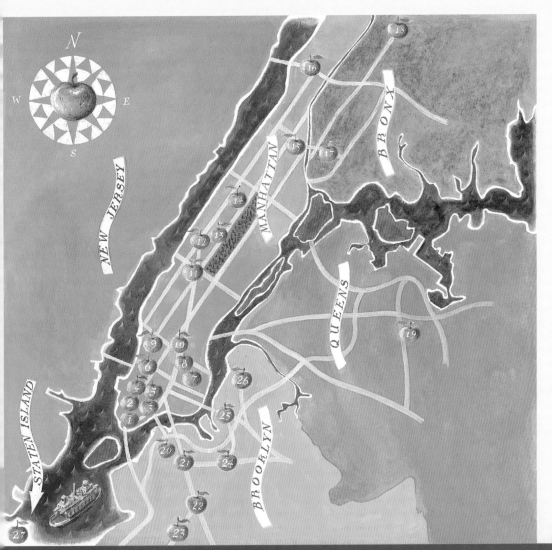

| | JAN | FEB | MAR | APR | MAY | JUN | JUL | AUG | SEP | OCT | NOV | DEC |
|---|---|---|---|---|---|---|---|---|---|---|---|---|
| **APPLES** | ● | ● | ● | ● | ● | ● | ● | ● | ● | ● | ● | ● |
| **APRICOTS** | | | | | | | ● | ● | ● | | | |
| **ARTICHOKES** | | | | | | | | ● | ● | | | |
| **ASPARAGUS** | | | | | ● | ● | | | | | | |
| **BEANS (SHELL)** | | | | | | | ● | ● | ● | | | |
| **BEANS (SNAP)** | | | | | | | ● | ● | ● | ● | | |
| **BEETS** | | | | | | | ● | ● | ● | ● | ● | |
| **BERRIES** *depending upon variety* | | | | | | ● | ● | | ● | | | |
| **BOK CHOY** | | | | | | ● | ● | | ● | ● | | |
| **BROCCOLI** | | | | | | | ● | ● | | ● | ● | ● |
| **BRUSSELS SPROUTS** | | | | | | | | | | ● | ● | ● |
| **CABBAGE** | ● | ● | | | | | ● | ● | | ● | ● | |
| **CARROTS** | ● | ● | ● | | | | ● | ● | ● | ● | ● | ● |
| **CAULIFLOWER** | | | | | | | ● | ● | | ● | ● | ● |
| **CELERIAC** | ● | ● | ● | ● | ● | | | | | ● | ● | ● |

| | JANUARY | FEBRUARY | MARCH | APRIL | MAY | JUNE | JULY | AUGUST | SEPTEMBER | OCTOBER | NOVEMBER | DECEMBER |
|---|---|---|---|---|---|---|---|---|---|---|---|---|
| CELERY | | | | | | | ● | ● | ● | ● | | |
| CHERRIES | | | | | | ● | ● | | | | | |
| CORN | | | | | | | ● | ● | ● | | | |
| CUCUMBERS | | | | | | | ● | ● | ● | ● | | |
| EGGPLANT | | | | | | | ● | ● | ● | ● | | |
| FIDDLEHEAD FERNS | | | | ● | | | | | | | | |
| FLORENCE FENNEL | | | | | | ● | ● | | ● | ● | | |
| FLOWERS | | | | | ● | ● | ● | ● | ● | ● | | |
| GARLIC | ● | ● | ● | ● | ● | ● | ● | ● | ● | ● | ● | ● |
| GRAPES | | | | | | | | | ● | ● | | |
| GREENS (COOKING) | | | | | | ● | ● | ● | ● | ● | ● | |
| GREENS (SALAD) | | | | | | ● | ● | ● | ● | ● | ● | |
| HERBS | ● | ● | ● | ● | ● | ● | ● | ● | ● | ● | ● | ● |
| HORSERADISH | ● | ● | ● | ● | ● | ● | ● | ● | ● | ● | ● | ● |
| HOUSEPLANTS | | | | | ● | ● | ● | ● | ● | ● | ● | ● |

|  | JAN | FEB | MAR | APR | MAY | JUN | JUL | AUG | SEP | OCT | NOV | DEC |
|---|---|---|---|---|---|---|---|---|---|---|---|---|
| **JERUSALEM ARTICHOKES** |  |  |  |  | ● | ● | ● | ● |  | ● | ● | ● |
| **KOHLRABI** |  |  |  |  |  | ● | ● | ● | ● | ● |  |  |
| **LEEKS** |  |  |  |  | ● | ● |  |  | ● | ● | ● | ● |
| **LETTUCES** |  |  |  |  | ● | ● | ● | ● | ● | ● | ● |  |
| **MELONS** |  |  |  |  |  |  |  | ● | ● |  |  |  |
| **MUSHROOMS** | ● | ● | ● | ● | ● | ● | ● | ● | ● | ● | ● | ● |
| **OKRA** |  |  |  |  |  |  |  | ● | ● | ● |  |  |
| **ONIONS** | ● | ● | ● | ● | ● | ● | ● | ● | ● | ● | ● | ● |
| **PARSNIPS** | ● | ● |  |  |  |  |  | ● | ● | ● | ● | ● |
| **PEACHES & NECTARINES** |  |  |  |  |  |  |  | ● | ● | ● |  |  |
| **PEARS** | ● |  |  |  |  |  |  | ● | ● | ● | ● | ● |
| **PEAS** |  |  |  |  |  | ● | ● |  | ● | ● |  |  |
| **PEPPERS** |  |  |  |  |  |  |  | ● | ● | ● | ● |  |
| **PLUMS** |  |  |  |  |  |  |  | ● | ● |  |  |  |
| **POTATOES** | ● | ● | ● | ● | ● | ● | ● | ● | ● | ● | ● | ● |

| | JANUARY | FEBRUARY | MARCH | APRIL | MAY | JUNE | JULY | AUGUST | SEPTEMBER | OCTOBER | NOVEMBER | DECEMBER |
|---|---|---|---|---|---|---|---|---|---|---|---|---|
| PUMPKINS | | | | | | | | | ● | ● | ● | |
| QUINCE | | | | | | | | ● | ● | ● | ● | ● |
| RADISHES | ● | ● | | ● | ● | ● | ● | ● | ● | ● | ● | ● |
| RAMPS | | | | | ● | | | | | | | |
| RHUBARB | | | | ● | ● | ● | ● | | | | | |
| SCALLIONS | | | | | | ● | ● | ● | ● | ● | ● | |
| SPINACH | | | | | | ● | ● | ● | ● | ● | ● | ● |
| SPROUTS & SHOOTS | | | | | ● | ● | | | | | | |
| SWEET POTATOES | ● | ● | ● | | | | | | ● | ● | ● | ● |
| TOMATILLOS & HUSK CHERRIES | | | | | | | ● | ● | ● | | | |
| TOMATOES | | | | | | | | ● | ● | ● | | |
| TURNIPS & RUTABAGAS | ● | ● | ● | ● | | | | ● | ● | ● | ● | ● |
| WATERMELON | | | | | | | | ● | ● | | | |
| WINTER SQUASH | ● | ● | ● | | | | | | ● | ● | ● | ● |
| ZUCCHINI & SUMMER SQUASH | | | | | | ● | ● | ● | ● | ● | | |

ENCYCLOPEDIA OF
# Greenmarket
# Produce

# APPLES

New York State, in general, and the Hudson River Valley, in particular, have been among America's primary apple-producing regions since the seventeenth century.

## VARIETIES

More than 50 varieties are available at Greenmarket, including:

**BALDWIN.** Tart, crisp, and juicy, it is an excellent all-purpose apple and is especially good for baking.

**CORTLAND.** Developed in Geneva, New York, this apple is tart and crisp. It tends to stay white, so is attractive in salads, and remains firm when baked.

**EMPIRE.** A McIntosh/Red Delicious cross, Empire was developed in the 1960s. More sweet than tart, it is also crisp and firm. Good for eating out of hand and in salads.

**GALA.** A bright red, juicy variety with a mild, sweet flavor and crisp yellow flesh.

**GOLDEN DELICIOUS.** A mild, sweet, juicy apple with light yellow flesh. Excellent for eating out of hand, in salads and sauces, and for baking.

**GRANNY SMITH.** Developed in the 1860s in Australia by Mrs. Anne Smith, this bright green apple is tart, crisp, and hard; perfect for eating out of hand, including in salads, and for baking.

**IDA RED.** A Jonathan/Wagner cross, it is tart, crisp, and firm. It stores well, and is a good all-purpose apple.

**JONAGOLD.** A Jonathan/Golden Delicious cross, it has a tangy, sweet flavor and is especially good for pies and sauces.

**JONATHAN.** Discovered in the 1820s in Woodstock, New York, it is a sweet, acidic apple that is excellent for eating raw, baking, and sauces.

**McINTOSH.** Developed in Canada in 1811, it is sweet, crisp, tender, and juicy. Good for eating out of hand, and in salads and sauces.

**MACOUN.** A McIntosh/Jersey cross, it is tart, crisp, and firm. Good for eating raw, baking, and sauces. It is the best-selling apple at Greenmarket.

**NORTHERN SPY.** Developed in upstate New York in the early 1800s, it is tart, crisp, yet tender. Considered by many to be the best all-purpose and baking apple.

**RED DELICIOUS.** Developed in the 1870s in Iowa, it is sweet, tender, and best for eating out of hand.

**ROME BEAUTY.** Found in the early 1800s in Ohio, it is sweet and firm. Because it holds its shape, it is good for baking and canning.

## SELECTING

Apples are at their most flavorful when they are just harvested, from late August through October. However, they hold up well in cold storage, and can be flavorful even in late February.

The color, whether crimson, yellow, or green, should be clear, bright, and relatively even. The apple should smell fresh, not musty, and should be firm with smooth skin devoid of bruises, nicks, or cuts. Apples may have "scalds" (brownish, dry areas), but these do not affect flavor and, in fact, indicate the apple's natural freshness.

## STORING

Store apples unwashed in a plastic bag in the refrigerator. Do not store apples next to broccoli, cabbage, cauliflower, cucumbers, greens, or lettuce; apples give off a gas that will hasten deterioration of these vegetables. This same gas helps to soften pears, peaches, and plums—simply place them in a paper bag with an apple.

## Putting Up

Apples may be canned, frozen, or preserved as butters, chutneys, or jellies. Apples are excellent dried. Apples can be put up in cold storage for several months.

## Preparing

For eating out of hand, apples need only be washed; the skin is edible, tasty, and provides fiber. Apples can be baked, microwaved, sautéed, and cooked down into a "butter" or sauce. To prepare for cooking, apples usually need to be peeled and cored.

## Serving Suggestions

Apples can be served raw or cooked, singly

or combined with other fruits, flavored or plain. Because they are naturally sweet, apples are often used in pies, cakes, cookies, quick breads, and other sweet baked goods. They can be dipped in caramel and served "candied" on a stick. Apples can be cooked into sauce, or sautéed and served with pork or game. Apples add crunch to salads, and combine beautifully with cheeses.

Apples are most delicious plucked from the tree and eaten out of hand.

---

### WALDORF SALAD
#### Serves 4

*This classic salad was developed by "Oscar," the legendary maitre d' at New York's Waldorf-Astoria Hotel.*

 2 firm ripe green apples, unpeeled, cored, and coarsely chopped
 1 firm ripe red apple, unpeeled, cored, and coarsely chopped
 1 tablespoon lemon juice
 1 cup chopped celery
 ½ cup coarsely chopped walnuts
 ½ cup mayonnaise
 2 tablespoons apple cider or juice
 1½ teaspoons honey
 1 head Bibb lettuce

Place the apples in a serving bowl and toss with lemon juice to coat. Add the celery and walnuts. Combine the mayonnaise, cider, and honey, and toss until the salad is thoroughly blended. Serve on a bed of Bibb lettuce.

---

W S S F

# FRED WILKLOW

## WILKLOW ORCHARDS
Ulster County • Highland, New York 12528
Stand at Borough Hall (Brooklyn)

*Fred wearing "the hat"*

Fred Wilklow is one of the best-loved farmers at Greenmarket. He and his brother, Frank, who moved to Louisiana a few years ago to go to medical school, began coming to market in June 1984. Since then, the Wilklow Orchards stand has been one of the highlights of the Borough Hall (Brooklyn) Greenmarket.

The 100-acre Wilklow Orchards has been a working farm for almost 150 years. Fred is the sixth generation of Wilklow to work the farm, and he hopes that one of his four children will carry on the tradition.

The primary crop at Wilklow Orchards is tree fruit, including apples, cherries, plums, apricots, peaches, and nectarines. As a result of this diversity, Fred is able to sell fruit every season of the year; even in winter the Wilklow stand features many apple varieties as well as hot cider.

In addition to the tree fruit, the Wilklows grow berries, corn, tomatoes, beans, lettuces, and greens. Several greenhouses are in operation, and beginning in mid-spring, the Wilklow stand features flowers, potted herbs, and bedding plants. Fred is also famous for bringing calves, piglets, and lambs from the farm to the market for kids to pet and feed. One Brooklyn customer even asked Fred to bring her raw wool after he had sheered his sheep, which she spun by hand into yarn and knitted a hat for Fred to wear during cold winter days at the market.

Greenmarket has had an enormous affect on Wilklow Orchards. Selling directly to consumers has allowed Fred to diversify and prosper. Loyal customers visit the Wilklow stand in Brooklyn regularly, and Fred and his wife, Sharon, are eager for New Yorkers to visit their farm, where they have a thriving pick-your-own business, a large farm stand, a cider mill, and a bakery.

# APRICOTS

Apricots are members of the peach family, although they are usually smaller and more delicate. They arrive at Greenmarket a few weeks earlier than their cousins, and make only a brief appearance. Despite their delicacy, they are filled with nutrients, especially beta carotene, which is why many commercially grown apricots are used in baby food.

## SELECTING
Like peaches, apricots will not ripen off the vine, so you must buy them ripe. Because they are so delicate, they are ripe for only a brief period. Look for a golden color, a round shape, and a slight give in texture (although not too soft). Avoid apricots with tan or brown bruises.

## STORING
Apricots keep for only a day or two. To soften them a bit, store them for 24 hours in a brown bag at room temperature. You can also store them in the crisper of your refrigerator.

## PUTTING UP
Apricots can be canned in syrup or preserved as jams, jellies, juices, or pickles. Apricots can be frozen in a sugar-pack (when they will be used for baking), or in syrup (if they will be served plain). Apricots can be dried, but it is an elaborate process, requiring special equipment.

## PREPARING

Apricots can be served raw, with or without the skin. Simply wash gently in cool water. If you need to peel the apricots, blanch them for about 15 seconds in boiling water, then gently peel off the skin with a sharp knife.

Since the flesh of the apricot will turn brown when exposed to the air, sprinkle it with lemon juice as you are preparing it.

## SERVING SUGGESTIONS

Apricots are best eaten out of hand at room temperature or sliced and sprinkled with with sugar. They are also particularly delicious stewed and served as a side dish or with dessert.

Apricots can be substituted for peaches or nectarines in virtually any recipe. Thus, like peaches, they are delicious served over ice cream, in yogurt, or with heavy cream. They make a delicious addition to quick breads, muffins, and pancakes, as well as cakes, pies, and tarts.

Apricots combine well with spices, especially cinnamon, nutmeg, and ginger. Poached or grilled apricots make an interesting side dish or garnish for grilled duck, roasted chicken, and baked ham.

---

### FROZEN APRICOT MOUSSE CASEY
#### Serves 6

*I have a Brooklyn-born cat named Casey who is precisely the color of apricot mousse. This recipe is dedicated to him.*

- 4 apricots, peeled, pitted, and sliced
- 2 egg whites
- ½ cup confectioners' sugar
- 2 cups heavy cream
- 2 teaspoons vanilla extract

Place the apricot slices in a blender or food processor and puree. Measure 1 cup of puree.

In a large bowl, beat the egg whites until foamy. Slowly adding ¼ cup of sugar, continue beating until the whites hold stiff peaks.

In another large bowl, whip the heavy cream until it forms soft peaks. Slowly adding the remaining ¼ cup sugar and the vanilla extract, continue beating until stiff.

Fold the egg whites into the whipped cream. Gently fold in the 1 cup of apricot puree and blend thoroughly. Spoon the mixture into a soufflé dish or mold and freeze.

Serve frozen.

---

# ARTICHOKES

Artichokes are not usually cultivated in our region, but in the past year or two a couple of Greenmarket farmers have grown them successfully. In fact, the local artichokes tasted so delicious that famed four-star chef Jean-Georges Vongerichten bought up most of them and offered them in his restaurants.

## VARIETIES

An artichoke is the unopened flower bud of a cousin of the thistle. Many varieties exist, but only the Green Globe, a round Italian type, is cultivated in North America. Artichokes vary in size, depending upon where on the stalk they grow: The largest grow on the center stalk; smaller buds on the side branches; and baby artichokes (which are not less mature artichokes, but a type of bud) develop at the base. Each artichoke consists of three parts: rubbery outer leaves, which often have sharp tips and tender bases; a choke, or thistle, which is enclosed within immature leaves; and a firm, succulent heart, or bottom.

## SELECTING

Choose well-shaped, tightly closed artichokes that are heavy for their size. The leaves should be fleshy, yet firm and crisp. Avoid artichokes that appear dry, cracked, or open, or have tiny holes in the stem, which indicate the presence of worms.

## STORING

Artichokes appear hardy, but are quite perishable. Store them in a plastic bag in the refrigerator for three or four days.

## PUTTING UP

Artichoke hearts can be canned, frozen, and pickled.

## PREPARING

Wash artichokes thoroughly under cool water. With a sharp noncarbon-steel knife, cut off the top half-inch of the bud, and

carefully trim the tips of the leaves. Rub the cut parts with lemon. Cut off the stem and remove any withered leaves at the base. Stand the artichokes upright in a pot or steamer, add a few inches of water, and boil or steam for 15 to 45 minutes depending upon the size. Remove the choke after cooking if the artichokes are to be stuffed. Baby artichokes have no choke, so simply wash, trim the stem and leaves, then slice.

## SERVING SUGGESTIONS

Serve artichokes as an appetizer whole and steamed with a dipping sauce (warm butter, lemon sauce, vinaigrette, etc.). Large artichokes can be stuffed with a variety of savory stuffings. Serve braised baby artichokes as an appetizer, a side dish, or as part of a pasta sauce.

### JEAN-GEORGES'S CURRIED ARTICHOKES
#### Serves 4

*This is how famed chef Jean-Georges Vongerichten prepares artichokes at his restaurants.*

4 to 6  baby artichokes
2  tablespoons butter or peanut oil
Salt to taste
About 1 teaspoon curry powder

Cut off the stems and top spikes, and trim the artichoke leaves, removing and discarding all the hard leaves and tips. Slice the artichokes as thinly as possible with a knife or a mandoline.

Heat the butter or oil in a 10-inch skillet over medium-high heat. Sprinkle the artichokes with salt and curry powder. When the butter foam subsides or when the oil is hot, add the artichokes and cook, shaking the pan a little bit from time to time, for 3 minutes. Add ¼ cup water to the skillet and continue to cook, shaking the pan occasionally, until the water has evaporated, about 5 to 10 minutes. Serve hot or at room temperature.

# ASPARAGUS

thin asparagus are best, but thicker, more mature spears can be just as delicious, especially when the stalks are peeled.

Occasionally a farmer will offer white asparagus, that is, asparagus that have been cultivated completely underground so they cannot produce chlorophyll. White asparagus tend to be more fibrous and less sweet.

Asparagus is the hoity-toity vegetable. Part of its distinction comes from the fact that it is relatively expensive due to its time-consuming cultivation. Not only does asparagus possess snob appeal, it contains a healthy dose of vitamins and minerals. And, joy of joys, it is a vegetable dieters can consume without guilt.

## SELECTING

At Greenmarket, asparagus begin to appear in late April and last through July. Look for spears that are firm yet tender, with deep green or purplish tips that are closed and compact. The stalks should be straight and have a rounded shape. Choose stalks that are the same size so that they cook evenly. Many people insist that pencil-

## STORING

Wrap stalks in a damp paper towel and place them in a plastic bag in the refrigerator crisper. Or place stalks in water, like flowers, cover tips with a plastic bag, and store in the refrigerator. Asparagus are almost as ephemeral as fresh corn, and should be kept chilled and consumed within two days.

## PUTTING UP

Asparagus do not can or dry well, although they can be nicely pickled. Asparagus freeze well; soak, blanch, and freeze like-sized spears together. Freeze ends for later use in soups and other cooked dishes.

## PREPARING

Cut or break off the tough ends of the spears. (Ends tend to break naturally at the point where the toughness ends and the tender part begins.) Wash the stalks thoroughly under cool water, making sure that all sand and dirt is removed, especially from the tips; soak them, if necessary.

Asparagus can be blanched, boiled, microwaved, or steamed. Use a pan that is large enough so the stalks need not be bent.

## SERVING SUGGESTIONS

Asparagus are at their best served lightly steamed. They are so flavorful that they do not require a rich sauce; instead, serve them with lemon juice, a light vinaigrette, chopped egg, peelings of good Parmesan, or a hint of butter. Asparagus can also be served cold, but should be blanched first to release their sweetness. Boil, steam, or stir-fry saved ends, and use them in sauces, stir-fries, quiches, and soups.

## ASPARAGUS ALFIO
### Serves 4

*Alfred Milanese, Greenmarket's pretzel man, created this dish for his grandfather, Alfio Vasi.*

| | |
|---|---|
| 1 | pound fresh asparagus |
| ¼ to ½ | cup olive oil |
| 1 | pound plum or globe tomatoes, peeled, chopped, and pureed |
| | Salt |
| | Freshly ground black pepper |
| 1 | pound tubular pasta, cooked al dente |

Wash, trim, and cut the asparagus into 1-inch lengths, separating the stalk ends from the tips. In a skillet, heat the olive oil over moderate heat. Add asparagus stalk ends and sauté for 5 minutes. Add tips, increase heat to high, and stir for 1 to 2 minutes. Reduce heat to medium, cover, and cook until the asparagus are tender, about 5 minutes. Uncover and add the tomatoes and salt and pepper to taste. Reduce heat to medium-low and cook for about 15 minutes more, or until the oil separates from the tomatoes. Pour the sauce over the cooked pasta, toss, and serve immediately.

# BAKED GOODS

Some of the most inventive bakeries in the region sell at Greenmarket, including the Rock Hill Bakehouse from Gansevoort, New York; Our Daily Bread from Chatham, New York; and Bread Alone from Boiceville, New York. Many farmers, like Fred Wilklow and Elizabeth Ryan, have also established their own line of baked goods.

## VARIETIES

**BREAD.** Several creative bread bakers sell many varieties of plain yeast breads as well as many less-traditional loaves.

**QUICK BREADS.** Cinnamon rolls, coffee cake, doughnuts, and muffins of all types are sold, many are sugar free and low fat.

**PIES, CAKES, & COOKIES.** Many farmers sell pies, cakes, and cookies made from fruits and vegetables grown on their land.

**FLOUR & GRAINS.** A couple of farmers sell cornmeal, wheat berries, and other grains that can be used for baking.

## STORING

Most breads and other baked goods will keep in the refrigerator or cupboard for at least three days if wrapped in plastic.

## PUTTING UP

Breads and pastries freeze well. Wrap the goods carefully in plastic wrap or put them in a freezer bag and quick freeze. Allow the baked goods to thaw in the wrapping before using or serving.

# TOM HALIK

JUST RUGELACH • Manhattan • New York, New York 10016

Stands at Washington Market Park, Federal Plaza, World Trade Center, and
Bowling Green (Manhattan); Borough Hall (Brooklyn); and St. George (Staten Island)

**B**aker Tom Halik is a graduate of the prestigious *École de Cuisine La Varenne* in Paris. After graduating in 1983, Tom was hired to be the chef at the United States Embassy in Reykjavík, Iceland, where he once cooked for President George Bush, among other heads of state.

Although working at an embassy was heady stuff, Tom ultimately returned to New Jersey, where he served as a chef at several restaurants, taught cooking classes, and cooked for various retail gourmet shops.

While cooking for Fifth Avenue Epicure, Tom was asked to come up with a special rugelach recipe. Rugelach reminded Tom of cookies his Slovenian grandmother used to make, so he worked up a recipe based on one of hers. It was a phenomenal success. Before long, Tom decided to go off on his own to see if he could make a living selling "just rugelach."

Tom rented kitchen space from a caterer who did not use his kitchen at night. From 6 P.M. until morning, Tom baked the rugelach himself, all by hand. After more than five years, Tom still does most of the cooking himself. He can prepare about 200 pounds of rugelach in a ten-hour shift, sleep for a few hours, bake the pastry, pack it, then go out and sell.

Tom began selling at Greenmarket five years ago, tucking his small stand into several locations. Although he also has a thriving wholesale and mail-order business, Tom especially likes the one-on-one relationships with Greenmarket customers. Still, he wonders what Anne Willan, directress of La Varenne, would think if she knew one of her former students was selling cookies on the street.

# BEANS

Beans can be divided into two basic categories: those with edible pods (green and other snap beans) and those that must be shelled (lima beans, fava beans, and soybeans, for example).

## VARIETIES

### Snap Beans

*Snap beans: green, yellow wax, and purple*

These beans, especially the classic green beans, are called snap beans because their crisp pods, which are edible, should "snap" when bent, an indication of freshness. (They are sometimes known as pod beans.) An interesting fact: Snap beans are closely related to kidney beans, which is why they are often combined in a classic bean salad.

**GREEN BEANS.** Once commonly known as string beans because early varieties had a long string down the pod seam that needed to be "zipped" off before cooking, these are the most common bean.

**YELLOW WAX BEANS.** A yellow variety of snap bean; the flavor is a bit sweeter than green beans.

**PURPLE WAX BEANS.** A purple snap

bean that turns green when cooked and tastes identical to its green-bean cousins.

**FRENCH BEANS.** Known also by their French name, *haricots verts*, these are slender, elegant beans with a sweet and sophisticated flavor.

**ROMANO BEANS.** Also known as Italian green beans, these beans are generally larger, broader, flatter, and somewhat sweeter than green beans.

**CHINESE LONG BEANS.** An Asian bean, and a close relative of the black-eyed pea, that is very long, thin, and mild-flavored; it makes an interesting side dish and a pretty addition to stir-fries.

## Shell Beans

These are called shell beans because they must be removed from their pods (or shells) before eating.

**FAVA BEANS.** Also called broad beans, these resemble giant lima beans with tough pods. These beans are often used in Mediterranean dishes.

**SOYBEANS.** These are an essential part of

Chinese cuisine, and are very nutritious. (Some farmers claim the pod can be eaten, at least on young soybeans.) This bland bean is used to make oil, tofu, flour, and milk. Soybeans can make a flavorful appetizer or side dish, and are best used as an ingredient in soups, stews, and casseroles.

**LIMA BEANS.** A well-known American

bean, especially in this region. They are pale green, plump, and bland-flavored, and come in two varieties, "baby limas," which are mild and tender, and the larger, more flavorful Fordhook limas.

**CRANBERRY BEANS** are so named because of the cranberry-red striations that appear on both the pod and the beans. The beans, when cooked, turn an unappetizing gray color, so are best used in soups, stews, and other dishes where the bean is disguised, and not as a side dish.

## SELECTING

**SNAP BEANS.** Choose beans that have fresh-smelling, brightly colored pods; avoid beans that are limp, withered, or spotted. They should "snap" when fresh.

**SHELL BEANS.** The beans should be in the pods and the pods should be plump, firm, and brightly colored.

## STORING

Store fresh snap beans, un-washed, in an airtight plastic bag in the refrigerator. They will keep two to three days. Store shell beans in their shells in a plastic bag in the refrigerator for up to a week. Shell just before using.

## PUTTING UP

**SNAP BEANS** can easily, and hundreds of recipes for canning and pickling are available. They can also be sun-dried, creating a bean known in the South as "Leather Britches." Snap beans can be frozen easily. To freeze: Trim and cut the beans into 4-inch lengths, wash them thoroughly, and blanch them for three minutes. Strain them in a colander, pack in an airtight container or plastic freezer bag, and freeze. Frozen beans will keep for about a year.

**SHELL BEANS** can, dry, and freeze easily and well. However, like peas, the commercial canned, dried, and frozen beans are so inexpensive and readily available, it is hardly worth the effort to do it yourself.

## PREPARING

**SNAP BEANS** should be washed, trimmed, then cut crosswise or diagonally into 3- to 4-inch lengths. (Beans can also be cut length-wise, or French-style, but this may cause them to lose their crispness.) Snap beans can be blanched, steamed, stir-fried, or cooked in the microwave. Avoid overcooking them, as they will lose their bright green color and marvelous crisp-tender texture.

**SHELL BEANS** must be removed from their pods before cooking. To shell, simply split the pod open and push out the beans with your thumb. (Mature fava beans must also have the skin removed from the beans themselves. To do so, split the skin with a sharp paring knife and slip it off.) Rinse the beans gently before cooking. Shell beans can be boiled, steamed, or microwaved.

## SERVING SUGGESTIONS

Both snap beans (especially traditional green beans) and shell beans are a favorite side dish. Both combine well with other vegetables (onions, garlic, and tomatoes, for example), fresh herbs, and nuts, especially almonds, walnuts, and pecans. They are always welcome on crudité platters and in salads, soups, stews, and casseroles.

## ALICE WATERS'S
## SUMMER BEAN RAGOUT
### Serves 6

*This lovely recipe is from Alice Waters's book*
*Chez Panisse Vegetables.*

- 1 pound fresh shell beans
  (cranberry, lima)
- 1 tablespoon olive oil
  Salt and freshly ground pepper
- 1 pound assorted snap beans
  (green, yellow wax, Romano)
- ¼ cup crème fraîche
- 1½ teaspoons finely chopped
  summer savory

Shell the shell beans and place in a saucepan
with enough water to cover them by about
1 inch. Add the olive oil and 1 teaspoon of
salt and bring to a boil. Reduce the heat and
simmer until the beans are tender, about 20
minutes. Remove from the heat and transfer
the beans and liquid to a shallow bowl to
cool. Keep the shell beans in their liquid
until ready to use.

While the shell beans are cooking, trim
the snap beans. Parboil them for 4 to 5 minutes until tender in a large pot of boiling,
salted water. (They should be cooked separately, according to variety, in order to
control cooking times.) Drain and spread
them out on paper towels to cool. Set aside.

Before serving, drain the shell beans and
put them in a large sauté pan with the snap
beans. Add about ¾ cup water and cook over
high heat until the beans are heated through
and the liquid has almost completely evaporated. Add the crème fraîche and savory and
continue cooking until the crème fraîche has
reduced a little and the beans are well coated.
Season to taste and serve.

*Cranberry beans*

# BEETS

Beets are like candy. True, they have not attained the popularity of a Hershey bar, but their sweetness can satiate even the most voracious sweet tooth. Even better, they are low in calories, high in vitamin C, and beautiful in color. What's not to like!

## VARIETIES

CHIOGGIA BEET. Also called a candy cane because it is striped red and white, this is a very sweet beet.

GARDEN BEET. Also called red beet because of its deep burgundy color, this is the most common beet.

*White sugar and Chioggia beets*

WHITE SUGAR BEET. A very sweet, Italian variety that is delicious blanched in salads. Because it is white, it doesn't bleed.

## SELECTING

Beets are available year-round. From June through October, they are at their peak, and baby beets are a special treat. Beets are usually sold with their greens attached, and young greens are delicious. Look for smooth, hard, round beets that are free of cuts, wrinkles, or bruises; the leaves should be small, crisp, and dark, although by fall they may be too large to be palatable.

## STORING

Cut off the greens before storing, leaving an inch of stem. Store the roots, unwashed, in a plastic bag in the refigerator; they will keep for three weeks. Store the greens, unwashed, in a plastic bag in the refrigerator; use them within three days.

## PUTTING UP

Beets can extremely well. (Some experts believe that beet color brightens with canning.) Beets also make delicious pickles and relishes. Beets do not freeze well; they cannot be dried.

*Garden beets*

## PREPARING

Prepare beets separately from other vegetables, as their juice tends to bleed. For many recipes, it may be easier to boil or steam the beets before peeling, chopping, or slicing. Cook beets with their skins on to preserve their color and nutrients.

To prepare, scrub the roots, rinse them, then boil or steam them until they can be pierced with a sharp knife, then peel them. Beets can also be baked or roasted, which intensifies their sweetness.

## SERVING SUGGESTIONS

Beets are the basis for Russian borscht and other soups. They make a flavorful side dish, and are delightful in salads and on crudité platters.

## MIXED SALAD WITH BEETS
### Serves 6

*This delicious salad tastes particularly wonderful with game, especially on an autumn day.*

- 3 medium beets
- ¼ cup cider vinegar
- 2 teaspoons Dijon mustard
- ¾ cup heavy cream
  Salt and freshly ground pepper
- 3 cups mild-flavored lettuce, such as Boston or Bibb
- 1 cup chopped beet greens
- 1 cup watercress
- 1 Belgian endive, chopped into bite-sized pieces
- 1 large apple, peeled, cored, and thinly sliced
- ¼ cup coarsely chopped walnuts

Boil the beets for about 1 hour, or until tender, then let cool, peel, and slice.

In a small bowl, whisk together the cider vinegar and the mustard. Slowly add the heavy cream, whisking constantly until the dressing is completely combined and smooth. Season with salt and pepper to taste.

Toss the greens, beets, apple, and walnuts together. Add the dressing, toss, and serve.

# BERRIES

Berries are among the most popular fruits. They are easy to eat (most can be enjoyed raw), and are versatile. In our region, berries come in many varieties. Raspberries, blueberries, and strawberries are perennial favorites, but many people prefer tarter fruits like blackberries.

*Blackberries and raspberries*

## VARIETIES

Many types of berries are available at Greenmarket, including:

**BLACKBERRIES.** Also known as bramble berries because they grow on a thorny bush, blackberries look like purple raspberries, although they are larger, firmer, and have a tarter flavor. (The darker the berry, the sweeter the flavor.) They have a relatively short growing season, and are most readily available in late June and July.

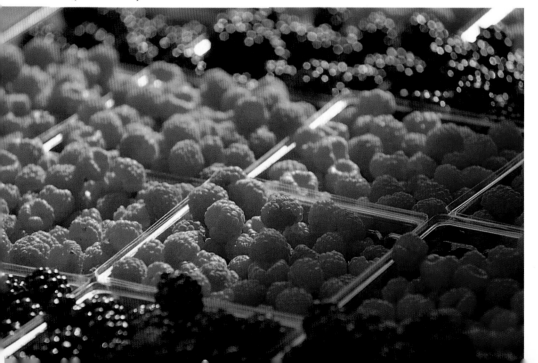

**BLUEBERRIES.** Dark, smooth, blue-skinned berries, blueberries are sturdier in texture (and thus provide more fiber) than most other berries. Blueberries are related to huckleberries and elderberries. Because they are sturdy, blueberries are perfect for salads and baked dishes.

**CURRANTS.** A small berry, related to the gooseberry, that comes in various colors, but usually only red is available. They make delicious jams, jellies, sauces, syrups, and flavored liqueurs.

**DEWBERRIES.** A cousin of the black-berry and raspberry, although smaller and sweeter and grow on a vine rather than a bush. Can be substituted for its relations in cooked recipes.

**GOOSEBERRIES.** Related to currants,  they are relatively un-common, but available with some farmers at Greenmarket. There are several varieties in many colors, but local gooseberries are pale green or yellow. Gooseberries must be cooked, as they do not have the sweetness and juiciness of other berries.

**HUCKLEBERRIES.** Dark blue or blue-black wild berries that are related to and closely resemble blueberries, although huckleberries are smaller, tarter, and firmer. They can be used in recipes instead of blueberries or elderberries.

**RASPBERRIES.** Like blackberries, rasp-berries are bramble berries and are extremely delicate. Most berry connois-seurs consider raspberries to be the most el-egant of the berries—perhaps because they are smaller, more fragile, and sweeter. Raspberries are also related to boysenberries, dewberries, loganberries, and youngberries, which are occasionally available at Green-market. Most cultivated raspberries are red, but some varieties are white, yellow, orange, and purple. Nevertheless, all varieties taste about the same. Raspberries first appear in June and July, then reappear (second pick-ing) briefly in September.

**STRAWBERRIES.** Strawberries are some-times called "false berries" because they grow from the base of the plant, not from the ovary of a flower. For more about strawberries, see page 224.

## SELECTING

Choose berries that are plump, dry, and firm, without signs of mold. Because berries are packed in boxes or baskets, it is sometimes difficult to discern if any are withered or decayed, but check the box for stains which can indicate spoilage. One pint serves two to three.

## STORING

Berries are delicate, and must be handled carefully. Before storing them, remove the berries from the box or basket (the farmer may have done this for you) and discard berries that are soft or overripe. Place the berries, unwashed, on a plate or a baking sheet lined with a paper towel to collect excess moisture, and cover with plastic wrap. Store in the refrigerator and serve within 24 hours.

*Currants flanked by blueberries*

## PUTTING UP

Whole berries freeze beautifully. Wash and drain them thoroughly, spread them on a baking sheet, freeze them, then transfer the frozen berries to a heavy plastic freezer bag. They will keep for a year. Most berries can also be frozen whole in syrup (wet-packed) or sugar (dry-packed), or pureed and then frozen for use in making sauces.

Berries can be preserved as juice, jam, jelly, and in some cases as flavoring in vinegars and oils. Most berries do not dry particularly well.

## PREPARING

Do not wash berries until just before using or serving them; washing can bruise them and hasten deterioration. Just before using, sort the berries and discard any that have become too soft, withered, or rotten.

Rinse the berries carefully under cold water, drain, and pat dry.

## SERVING SUGGESTIONS

The most sumptuous way to serve berries—especially raspberries— is raw as a "solo act," in a large crystal bowl, possibly sprinkled lightly with granulated or confectioners' sugar. Berries also combine beautifully with their close relations (blackberries and raspberries; blueberries and huckleberries) in a compote, or with other fruits, especially peaches, nectarines, and apricots, in a fruit dessert. Add a dash of dry sparkling wine, Champagne, or a fruit-flavored liqueur for an extra treat.

Some berries, especially raspberries and blueberries, can be added to wine vinegar and certain cooking oils for flavoring.

Berries make a delicious dessert served over yogurt, ice cream, sherbet, or frozen mousse. If your berries look a bit tired, make a sauce by pureeing them and flavoring with sugar or a liqueur.

Berries also are wonderful served over cereal and in pancakes, scones, muffins, and other quick breads. They can be used in infinite ways in cakes, pies, tarts, puddings, soufflés, and mousses.

---

### JEAN-GEORGES'S WARM FRUIT COMPOTE
#### Serves 4

*This recipe is from Jean-Georges's* Cooking at Home with a Four Star Chef, *and is a wonderful and easy dessert.*

- ½ cup sugar, more or less depending on the sweetness of the berries
- 3 tablespoons butter
- 2 cups huckleberries, currants, raspberries, blueberries, or other fruit, peeled, hulled, picked over, washed, and dried

  Crème fraîche or sour cream

Combine ½ cup water with the sugar and butter in a thick-bottomed saucepan and cook over medium-high heat, stirring until the mixture is syrupy, but not browned.

Toss in the fruit and cook over low heat until the fruit begins to break up and release its juices, about 2 minutes (some fruits will require the addition of a little more water). Serve topped with a bit of crème fraîche or sour cream (thinned with heavy cream, if necessary).

---

# Bok Choy & Napa Cabbage

Both bok choy and napa cabbage are, at times, referred to as "Chinese cabbage," but, although related, they should not be confused with one another. Still, they are both tasty and very nutritious.

## Varieties

Bok choy (also called Chinese white cabbage and white mustard cabbage) looks like a cross between celery and lettuce. The wide celery-like stalks are white and the leaves are bright green. The leaves have a bitter flavor, while the stalks are mild. A popular variety is Shanghai, or baby, bok choy.

Napa cabbage (also called celery cabbage or Peking cabbage, among several other names) looks like a tightly closed head of lettuce, only much paler green. (The leaves are white at the bottom, and pale green, tender, and curly at the top.) Napa cabbage is more delicate and crispy than standard cabbage, almost like a cross between lettuce and cabbage.

## Selecting

Choose bright, crisp, tightly packed heads. Select the large-leaved mature heads for making dishes where the leaves will be shredded or cooked.

## Storing

Store both varieties, unwashed, in a plastic bag in the vegetable crisper of the refrigerator. They will keep for three days.

## Putting Up

Both bok choy and napa cabbage can be frozen as part of a soup. Bok choy makes delicious pickles.

## Preparing

To prepare bok choy, trim the base and slice the leaves from stalks, leaving as little green as possible. Gently pull apart the ribs and flush away any sand. Prepare and cook stems and leaves separately. With baby bok choy, halve or quarter the heads lengthwise. To prepare napa cabbage, wash, and cook like other cabbages.

## SERVING SUGGESTIONS

Serve young bok choy and shredded napa cabbage in salads and slaws. Both bok choy and napa cabbage can be steamed, boiled, braised, microwaved, stuffed, or stir-fried. Both, of course, are delicious in Asian dishes, especially soups and stir-fries.

### SHANGHAI BOK CHOY
#### Serves 4

*This is a variation on a recipe created by the gifted cook Eileen Yin-fei Lo.*

    4  heads (about 1½ pounds) baby bok choy, washed and trimmed
    4  cups water
  ½  teaspoon baking soda
    1  teaspoon salt
    2  tablespoons peanut oil
    1  clove garlic, minced
    1  tablespoon chicken stock

For the sauce, combine in a bowl:

    2  teaspoons oyster sauce
  ½  teaspoon dark soy sauce
  ½  teaspoon sugar
  ½  teaspoon Chinese wine or sherry
    2  teaspoons cornstarch
  ½  cup cold water

Cut each head of bok choy lengthwise into quarters. Heat water in a wok or saucepan to boiling. Add baking soda and salt, and blanch the bok choy for 2 minutes. Drain.

Heat a wok over high heat, add oil. When a wisp of smoke appears, add garlic and cook about 30 seconds. Add the stock and bok choy and stir-fry for 1 minute. Add the sauce, and stir-fry until warmed through. Serve.

# BROCCOLI

The name "broccoli" comes from the Latin *brachium,* which means "arm" and refers to its pretty, tree-like shape. It is a member of the Brassica family, which includes other strongly flavored vegetables such as cabbage. Broccoli is rich in nutrients, especially beta carotene, vitamin C, and nitrogen compounds called indoles, which can protect against certain forms of cancer.

## SELECTING

Broccoli is at its most flavorful when it is young; mature broccoli can be tough and have a strong, cabbagy odor when cooked. Look for broccoli with slender, crisp stalks. The florets should be tightly closed and bright to dark green; any sign of yellow indicates that the broccoli has lost its nutritional value. Broccoli that is very dark green or purplish is even more nutritious. Avoid broccoli with brown spots or any sign of sliminess.

## STORING

Store broccoli, unwashed, in a perforated plastic bag in the crisper of the refrigerator. Broccoli is at its best if used within a day or two, but will keep for up to three or four days in the refrigerator.

## PUTTING UP

Broccoli does not can well, often turning brown, soft, and strong-flavored. It cannot be dried.

Broccoli freezes beautifully, and should be frozen when it is young and fresh to preserve the most flavor and crispness. To freeze, trim the stalks, then blanch them in scalding water for about three minutes, instantly immerse them in ice water, pack them in freezer containers or bags, and freeze. It will keep for about a year.

Take a few minutes when preparing fresh broccoli to freeze the extra-nutritious stems that you were probably about to throw away. Use them later in stir-fries, salads, casseroles, quiches, purees, and soups.

## PREPARING

Wash broccoli thoroughly in cold water to remove dirt. If the florets seem sandy, soak the stalks in cold water for about 30 minutes. If you wish, remove the leaves that cling to the stalks, although the leaves are tasty and contain high quantities of beta carotene and vitamin C. Clip the florets into bite-sized pieces or serve the broccoli in stalks.

Broccoli can be blanched, baked, boiled, steamed, microwaved, and stir-fried.

## SERVING SUGGESTIONS

Broccoli is an ideal side dish when served with mild-flavored meats such as chicken and veal.

Broccoli florets make attractive additions to salads, stir-fries, and pasta dishes. Broccoli can also be pureed to make a hearty cream soup.

Broccoli is delicious as a crudité, but it should be blanched for about two minutes and then chilled before serving.

Many cookbooks suggest serving broccoli with a cheese sauce, but it is equally delicious (and less fattening) with just a dab of butter or with a sprinkling of fresh lemon juice.

# BRUSSELS SPROUTS

Brussels sprouts are members of the cabbage family, and look like tiny heads of cabbage. They may have originally been cultivated in Belgium, and thus the origin of their name. Brussels sprouts have a strong, cabbagy taste, but a denser texture. Like cabbage, they can turn bitter or mushy when cooked. In this region, Brussels sprouts are available in late fall.

## SELECTING

At Greenmarket, Brussels sprouts are available both loose, so you can select each sprout individually, or attached to the stalk, which is how they grow. Choose sprouts that are bright green, with fresh-looking leaves. Avoid sprouts with yellowed or wilted leaves. The tastiest sprouts are small, tight, and compact; not soft or puffy.

## STORING

Store sprouts, unwashed, in a plastic bag in the refrigerator until ready to use. If they are on the stalk, allow them to remain so until you are ready to prepare them. They will keep for about four days.

## PUTTING UP

Brussels sprouts do not can well; they become soggy and strong flavored. They can be frozen, but should be picked over carefully and blanched before freezing. Brussels sprouts can be pickled.

## PREPARING

Allow Brussels sprouts to soak for a few minutes in warm water to force out sand or insects; then rinse them thoroughly. Trim the ends, and, with a sharp paring knife, put a small nick, or a cross, in the base so that the sprouts cook evenly. Brussels sprouts can be boiled, steamed, braised, or cooked in the microwave oven.

## SERVING SUGGESTIONS

Brussels sprouts are strong-flavored vegetables, so they work best as a side dish or as part of salad (blanch them first for about one minute) rather than as a main ingredient or flavoring. Even as a side dish, they can overwhelm the flavor of a mild chicken dish or a poached fish. On the other hand, Brussels sprouts are delicious with game (they are traditionally served with Thanksgiving turkey), beef, and ham.

Brussels sprouts combine well with strong-flavored cheeses (Cheddar, Monterey Jack, Gruyère, Parmesan); many herbs (dill, fennel, tarragon); spices (cinnamon, nutmeg, allspice); flavorings (lemon, mustard, vinegar); nuts (almonds, chestnuts, walnuts, pecans); and seeds (sesame, caraway, poppy).

## SAUTÉED BRUSSELS SPROUTS WITH MUSTARD SEEDS
### Serves 4 to 6

*Larry Forgione, famed chef of An American Place in Manhattan and 1776 Tavern at the Beekman Arms in Rhinebeck, New York, is a devotee of Greenmarket. This is his recipe.*

2  pints small Brussels sprouts
2  tablespoons salted butter
2  teaspoons yellow mustard seeds
2  tablespoons whole-grain mustard
½  teaspoon salt
    Freshly ground black pepper

Trim the bottoms from the sprouts and cut a small cross in the base of each.

Bring a large pot of salted water to a boil, add the sprouts, and cook for 5 to 8 minutes, until tender but still slightly firm. Drain.

Heat the butter in a large skillet over medium heat until it foams and turns light brown. Add the mustard seeds and cook, stirring, over low heat for 1 minute. Add the cooked sprouts and toss gently. Stir in the mustard, salt, and pepper to taste and cook for 1 minute more. Spoon the sprouts into a serving dish and serve immediately.

# CABBAGE

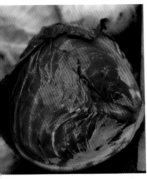

Cabbage lost a bit of its popularity in recent years, but we should remember that it is flavorful, low in calories, high in nutrients, and very versatile. Best of all, it can be found at Greenmarket well into the winter.

*Red cabbage with green cabbage*

## VARIETIES

**GREEN CABBAGE.** Perhaps the most common variety, green cabbage comes in tight heads with pale green outer leaves and even paler green or white inner leaves.

**RED CABBAGE.** Similar in flavor but a bit tougher than green cabbage, red cabbage has dark red to purple outer leaves with white streaks.

**SAVOY CABBAGE.** A green cabbage with more crinkly leaves and a looser head, Savoy has a milder flavor and more delicate texture than other varieties.

## SELECTING

Choose cabbage with fresh, crisp, tightly packed leaves; avoid heads with loose outer leaves, although Savoy cabbage is more loosely packed. The head should be heavy for its size. Avoid cabbage with dull, withered leaves or brown spots.

## STORING

Store cabbage, unwashed, in a plastic bag in the refrigerator. It will keep for ten days.

## PUTTING UP

Cabbage can be canned as sauerkraut and pickled in vinegar, but both these processes work best only in large quantities. Cabbage can be frozen, but loses its crispness. It holds up for months stored in a root cellar.

*Savoy cabbage*

## Preparing

Remove withered leaves. To cut, use a stainless-steel knife because carbon steel will leave black smudges on the leaves. (Similarly, do not cook cabbage in an aluminum or cast-iron pot.) If the cabbage is to be served in wedges, leave the core intact to hold the leaves in place. If it is to be cut up, core it, quarter it, slice it vertically, or shred it with a hand shredder or in a food processor. Savoy cabbage can be torn like lettuce. To preserve nutrients, do not wash the cabbage until after it has been cut or shredded. Wash leaves gently under cool water and pat them dry.

Cabbage can be boiled, steamed, braised, stir-fried, or cooked in the microwave.

## Serving Suggestions

Cabbage is the primary ingredient in coleslaw, and a classic accompaniment to corned beef or pork. It combines well with potatoes, rice, and other grains, and is also delicious in soups and stews.

Cabbage is often used as a wrapper, and stuffed with rice, barley, chopped vegetables, fruits, or ground meat, as in many middle European, Middle Eastern, and Asian dishes.

---

### RED CABBAGE WEDGES WITH HORSERADISH BUTTER
#### Serves 6 to 8

*This dish was created by my friend John Hadamuscin, and appeared in his wonderful book* Special Occasions.

- 1 cup water
- ¼ cup cider vinegar
- 1 head red cabbage, uncored, cut into 6 wedges

For the butter:

- 2 tablespoons butter, softened
- 1 tablespoon prepared horseradish
- 1 tablespoon coarse-grained mustard

---

Pour the water and vinegar into a saucepan fitted with a steamer rack, place over high heat, and bring to a boil. Place the cabbage on the rack, cover, and steam for 10 to 12 minutes, or until crisp-tender. Arrange the wedges on a serving platter.

In a small bowl, beat together the butter, horseradish, and mustard until well blended. Slather the horseradish butter on the warm cabbage, or pass it separately.

# CARROTS

Carrots are often taken for granted, although they are beautiful, tasty, and very sociable. They are members of the Umbelliferae family, and, in earlier incarnations, were daintier and purple in color; only within the last 200 years have they been bred to their present orange hue.

## SELECTING

Almost all the carrots at Greenmarket are sold with tops attached, and they should be bright green and crisp. The roots should be well-shaped, straight, and devoid of dried rootlets. Avoid carrots that are cracked, shriveled, or limp. The color should be bright orange, not pale, since the darker the color, the greater the amount of beta carotene. Baby carrots are sweet and tender, but very large carrots can be even sweeter, as long as the core is not wide and woody.

## STORING

Twist off the green tops before storing. (The tops will wilt and draw moisture from the carrots, making them limp.) Store carrots in a plastic bag in the refrigerator crisper. Carrots will keep for at least two weeks, and much longer if they are to be used in cooked dishes.

## PUTTING UP

Carrots can well. They become soggy when frozen whole or sliced; however, carrot puree freezes extremely well, and makes an excellent base for soups and sauces. Carrots can be preserved as pickles, relish, and marmalade. They cannot be dried. Carrots can be stored in a root cellar for six months.

## PREPARING

To prepare carrots for cooking, scrub them thoroughly and peel with a vegetable peeler. Carrots can be steamed, microwaved, or baked. Cooking carrots brings out their sweetness; for brighter color, add a bit of beet juice to the cooking water. To prepare raw carrots, wash, peel, and slice them, then blanch them for one minute, which makes them brighter, sweeter, and easier to digest.

## Serving Suggestions

Enjoy carrots raw, or add them to green salads, slaws, and sandwich spreads or fillings. Cooked carrots are included in an infinite number of sauces (including classic tomato sauces) to provide natural sweetness. They also add color and sweetness to soups, meat loaves, casseroles, quick breads, and baked goods. Carrots combine beautifully with other vegetables, including potatoes, beans, and peas. In fact, for a change, try carrot disks and sugar snap peas instead of traditional peas and carrots.

## ROASTED CARROTS WITH HERBS
**Serves 4 to 6 as a side dish**

*This recipe allows the carrots to "slow-cook," giving them a wonderful earthy flavor that combines beautifully with roast pork or lamb.*

| | |
|---|---|
| 1 | pound carrots, peeled and thinly sliced on the diagonal |
| 2 | tablespoons butter |
| ½ | cup chicken stock |
| 1 | teaspoon chopped fresh basil |
| 2 | tablespoons chopped fresh parsley |
| ½ | teaspoon salt |
| | Coarsely ground black pepper |
| | Chopped fresh basil or parsley, for garnish |

Preheat the oven to 375°F. Arrange the sliced carrots in a buttered shallow baking dish and dot with butter. Combine the stock, herbs, salt, and pepper to taste in a measuring cup. Pour the stock mixture over the carrots, cover, and roast, turning once or twice, until the vegetables are very tender, about 50 minutes. Serve hot, garnished with chopped basil or parsley.

# CAT GRASS

Cat grass is young wheat or barley grass, but is known as "cat" grass because it was developed to be sold to urban cat owners whose felines do not have access to fresh grass. Cats seek out grass to help stimulate digestion and cleanse their systems of hair balls. Also, like most creatures of nature, cats want to supply their bodies with chlorophyl and other nutrients, which grass provides.

Some cats love cat grass, some don't, and still others will consume it voraciously at certain times and ignore it at others. (As cat owners know, cats know what they need when they it.)

 Wheat grass (or barley grass for those who are allergic to wheat) can be a welcome nutritional addition to the human diet and is reputed to retard certain cancers. At Greenmarket, wheat grass is sold as juice, and must be drunk on the spot. It has a very strong, pungent, grassy flavor.

## SELECTING

Cat grass is grown indoors under lights by several farmers and is sold throughout the year at Greenmarket. (Natural baby wheat grass is available only during the early spring.) Cat grass is available in pots or flats of various sizes. Look for bright green, fresh shoots.

## STORING

Treat cat grass as you would a houseplant or a potted herb. It requires medium sunlight and should be watered every two or three days. It will keep for weeks, depending upon the cat's (or the human's) gastronomical requirements.

## PREPARING AND SERVING

For cats, the grass pot can be placed with other houseplants (the cat will find it naturally), put next to the pet's feeding dish, or chopped and mixed in with the pet's food.

For humans, cat grass can be added to salads, soups, casseroles, or any other dish as you would any herb.

CAT GRASS
IS
WHEATGRASS
Greener Pastures™
Monticello, N.Y.

## STEWART BOROWSKY

**GREENER PASTURES FARM** • Orange County
Monticello, New York 12701
Stand at Union Square (Manhattan)

Stewart Borowsky works a small, six-acre farm outside Monticello, New York. Most of his land is wooded and thus not suited to cultivation, but during the summer and autumn months he does sell organic sprouts, lettuce, spinach, tomatoes, pumpkins, and sunflowers at Greenmarket. However, Stewart is best known at the Union Square Greenmarket for his Pet Patch™, the flats of cat grass he sells year-round to Greenmarket cat lovers.

The son of biologists, Stewart drove trucks and other heavy equipment, particularly farm equipment, before becoming a farmer. While living out West, he worked on a permaculture farm, and thus became interested in organic farming. When he returned to the Northeast, he worked briefly on a trout farm and then began cultivating his own land.

Working at Union Square on Mondays, Wednesdays, Fridays, and Saturdays next to his signature yellow school bus, Stewart operates his small stand. In front of the stand is a huge board entitled "The Pet Patch Hall of Fame," with photographs of the feline pets ("pre-furred customers") of local New York shoppers. Each week he features a "Cat of the Week," and encourages neighbors to bring pictures of their pets. Of course, Stewart has a cat of his own, a large white male named Sherlock.

# CAULIFLOWER

At some point cooks noticed that if they didn't boil cauliflower to death, it had a deliciously crisp, almost meaty texture and an interesting flavor. Recently, several New York chefs have met with raves when they featured cauliflower on their menus.

## VARIETIES

A few Greenmarket farmers are experimenting with cauliflower varieties:

BROCCOFLOWER, a hybrid of broccoli and cauliflower, is a chartreuse-colored vegetable with a subtle, mild flavor.

ROMANESCA, a lime-green variety with cone-like rather than round florets, it was originally bred in Italy and has a mild flavor.

## SELECTING

Choose cauliflower with tightly packed, milky white florets and fresh, green leaves devoid of brown spots or withering. For pale green varieties, look for a clear, bright color. Cauliflower should smell fresh and faintly cabbagy.

## STORING

Store cabbage, unwashed and tightly wrapped in plastic wrap, in the refrigerator. It will keep for about five days.

## PUTTING UP

Canning is possible, but the process intensifies cauliflower's flavor, softens its crispy texture, and yellows its florets. Cauliflower pickles nicely. Freezing makes the florets rubbery, so freezing as a puree or soup is recommended. Drying is not possible.

Cauliflower can be kept in cold storage for up to eight weeks.

## PREPARING

Remove withered leaves. Core the cauliflower with a sharp knife, break the florets gently, and steam or blanch them. Alternatively, some cooks recommend cooking the head whole in an uncovered pot.

To sweeten the flavor and preserve the whiteness, soak the head in cold water for 30 minutes before cooking, and add the lemon juice, white vinegar, or milk to the cooking water.

## SERVING SUGGESTIONS

Cauliflower can be served raw or briefly blanched in a salad or as part of a crudité platter. For a side dish, cauliflower can be boiled or steamed until tender but still crisp and served with a butter or cheese sauce, or cooked until soft and then pureed. (Some chefs serve caviar atop cauliflower puree.) Cauliflower puree can be thinned for soup, or it combines well with many cheeses, especially Swiss, Gruyère, and Cheddar in a casserole. Cauliflower can be deep-fried for an appetizer or side dish.

---

### MOST VOLUPTUOUS CAULIFLOWER
### Serves 4

*Anne Rosensweig serves this recipe at her fabulous restaurant, The Lobster Club.*

- 1 head cauliflower, cut into florets
- 2 tablespoons unsalted butter
- 1½ cups heavy cream
- 1½ cups grated Gruyère cheese
  Salt and freshly ground black pepper
- ¼ cup mascarpone cheese
- ½ cup freshly grated Parmesan cheese

---

Preheat the oven to 450°F. Steam cauliflower until crisp-tender, 3 to 5 minutes.

In a heavy saucepan over low heat, heat the butter, cream, and 1 cup of the Gruyère until bubbling. Season with salt and pepper to taste. Add the cauliflower and heat for 2 minutes.

Spread the cauliflower in a 2-quart baking dish. Sprinkle with the remaining Gruyère, dot with the mascarpone, and sprinkle with the Parmesan. Bake for 1 minute. Increase heat to broil, and broil until the surface is golden brown, 1 to 2 minutes. Serve immediately.

# CELERIAC

Celeriac is a ball-shaped root vegetable that tastes much like celery, but with a stronger, more concentrated flavor. Known also as celery root, it is not, as is sometimes thought, the root of the common celery plant.

## SELECTING

Look for small (no larger than a baseball), heavy-for-their-size, firm roots free of deep cuts or soft spots. Stems and leaves (which are not eaten but can be used to flavor soups) should be fresh and green.

## STORING

Store celeriac in a plastic bag in the vegetable crisper of the refrigerator. It will keep for as long as two weeks.

## PUTTING UP

Celeriac can be frozen, but first it must be scrubbed, cut into cubes or slices, then blanched for 3 or 4 minutes. Pack in freezer bags or containers and freeze.

## PREPARING

Peel the root with a vegetable peeler and use a very sharp blade of a food processor to slice or julienne. Some cookbooks recommend blanching the root either before it is peeled and sliced (for about 30 minutes), or after it has been peeled and sliced (8 to 10 minutes). However, many cooks believe that blanching takes the crispness out of the root and affects its flavor.

## SERVING SUGGESTIONS

Celery root is delicious as an hors d'oeuvre, either as part of a crudité platter or as classic *celeri rémoulade*. It is also delicious cooked and used in salads or as a side dish. Its spicy flavor combines well with cheese, cream, and meat.

## CELERI RÉMOULADE
### Serves 2 to 4

*Esteemed food editor, Narcisse Chamberlain, spent most of her childhood in France. While living there, her family was blessed with a wonderful French cook whom Narcisse's father fictionalized in his 1943 book* Clementine in the Kitchen. *This recipe is from that book.*

    1   small to medium celeriac,
        about 1 pound
    1   hard-boiled egg
    1   raw egg yolk
    1½  teaspoons Dijon mustard
        Salt and freshly ground pepper
    2   tablespoons tarragon vinegar
    ½   cup cold olive oil
        Minced parsley and chives

Trim and peel off all the fibrous material and skin from the surface of the celery root. Cut into large chunks, then, using a very sharp vegetable shredder or the julienne disk of a food processor, julienne the chunks into uniform ⅛-inch strips. You should have about 2 cups of julienned strips.

In a medium-sized bowl, mash together the hard-boiled egg and the raw egg yolk. Add the mustard, salt and pepper to taste, and vinegar, and work the mixture into a smooth paste. Slowly add the olive oil, whisking constantly, until the sauce thickens to the consistency of mayonnaise. (You can make the dressing very quickly in a blender.)

Toss the celery root with the sauce and chill. Garnish with minced parsley and chives just before serving.

# CELERY

Celery is one of those vegetables we all take for granted. We stroll right by it in the supermarket and almost without thinking, reach out, grab the bag, and toss it in our cart. However, comparing fresh-from-the-farm Greenmarket celery with supermarket celery is rather like comparing a pizza from the corner greasy spoon with a pizza from Spago. Grocery-store celery is a little too perky, a little too flashy, and most of all, tasteless. Greenmarket celery is earthy, with a remarkable peppery flavor.

Finally, a few words about the grammar of celery: A "bunch" of celery is actually a "stalk," while what most of us call a "stalk" is actually a "rib." The "celery heart"—the best part of the celery—is the cluster of small ribs closed tightly within the stalk. Some people confuse the heart with celeriac, or celery root, which is only a distant relative. (See page 76.)

## SELECTING
Choose celery with bright green ribs and a glossy surface. The bunch (that is, the stalk) should be compact, tight, and well-shaped. The leaves should be brightly colored, fresh-looking, and crisp, and the leaf stems should snap. Avoid if ribs show signs of bruising or rotting.

## STORING
Store celery in a plastic bag, with a sprinkling of water, in the vegetable crisper of the refrigerator. It will keep for two weeks. Don't permit celery to freeze, which it will do easily since it is made up primarily of water. Freezing damages the walls of the celery's cells, and when it is defrosted, the ribs will be limp. To refresh slightly wilted celery, separate the ribs, cut off the ends, and submerge in ice water for about 30 minutes.

## PUTTING UP

Like all vegetables that are composed primarily of water, celery does not can or freeze well because it loses its crispness. However, celery can be canned (using the hot-pack method) or frozen, and still retain its flavor for later use in cooked dishes. Celery leaves can be dried and used as celery flavoring, as you would with dried herbs.

## PREPARING

Wash celery thoroughly to remove sand and dirt. Cut, chop, or mince, according to the recipe. Celery can be braised, boiled, stir-fried, baked, or microwaved.

## SERVING SUGGESTIONS

Celery is an integral part of many sauces and casseroles. Fresh raw celery can provide the crunch in salads and crudité platters. Cooked celery can be served as a side dish or a soup.

### CELERY VASI
**Serves 4**

*This wonderful recipe was developed by Alfred Milanese, the sponsor of Martin's Homemade Pretzels at Greenmarket.*

1   bunch of fresh celery
    Olive oil
1   teaspoon lemon juice
½   cup freshly grated Parmesan cheese
    Salt and freshly ground black pepper

Wash and thinly slice celery into ½-inch diagonal strips. In a skillet, heat the olive oil over high heat and sauté the celery, stirring for about 5 minutes. (It's okay to brown the edges.) Reduce heat, cover, and cook until the celery is softened, about 5 more minutes. Uncover, sprinkle with lemon juice, add salt and several grindings of black pepper, then turn heat to high and stir for 1 to 2 minutes. Turn celery into a warm bowl and toss with the grated Parmesan. Serve immediately.

# CHEESE

*Sheep's milk cheeses*

In recent years, an explosion in the number of small, artisanal cheese producers has occurred in the United States. Several producers, including such prize-winning cheesemakers as Coach Farm, Little Rainbow Chèvre, and the Old Chatham Sheepherding Company, are regular sellers at Greenmarket.

Cheeses sold at Greenmarket must be made by the farmer who sells them. The farmer must have a dairy herd (cows, goats, or sheep) that produces at least 60 percent of the milk used to make a single milk cheese; the other 40 percent must come from a local farmer.

Generally, cheeses fall into two categories: unripened (or fresh), and ripened (or aged). Among the most familiar fresh, unripened cheeses are cottage cheese, cream cheese, pot cheese, ricotta, and simple cheese curds.

To ripen (or age) cheese, the curds are treated in a numbers of ways, including adding bacteria, heating, soaking, flavoring, coloring, pressing, and aging. Cheeses are then broken down into additional categories such as hard cheeses (Parmesan), semi-firm (Cheddar), semi-soft (Gouda), soft-ripened (Brie), blue-veined (Roquefort), and spun paste or pasta filata (mozzarella).

## VARIETIES

The following types of cheese are sold at Greenmarket:

**CHEESE CURDS.** Plain cheese curds can be eaten as a snack or used in cooking.

**COW'S MILK CHEESES.** A number of traditional cow's milk cheeses are available including Cheddar, Jack, and Camembert.

**GOAT'S MILK CHEESES.** Fresh goat's milk cheese, or chèvre, is the unripened curd of goat's milk. It is chalky white and has a flaky texture and a mild flavor that carries other flavors well. It comes in many shapes. Ripened goat's milk cheeses (often aged with the addition of a penicillin mold)

*Goat cheese buttons*

form a white rind similar to the rind found on Brie. Ripened goat's milk cheeses are creamier than chèvre, but not as smooth as Brie. They come in cones, pyramids, and disks, and are sometimes flavored with herbs or spices.

**RICOTTA.** A fresh cheese made from cow's, goat's, or sheep's milk. So-called Old World, or Italian, ricotta, made from the whey of sheep's milk, is also available.

**SHEEP'S MILK CHEESES.** Less than ten years ago, no sheep's milk cheese was made in the United States. Although cheesemakers in other countries have been making sheep's milk cheeses for centuries (Italian ricotta, pecorino, and Roquefort are three famous examples), American shepherds could raise sheep only for wool or meat and were prohibited by law from using sheep's milk for commercial purposes. Thanks to a change in the law, sheep's milk

can now be used to make cheese as well as other products, such as yogurt.

Fresh sheep's milk cheese resembles chèvre in appearance, but is smoother and has a stronger flavor. Sheep's milk cheese comes in wheels, buttons, and pyramids, and is sometimes seasoned or flavored with spices or herbs.

*East Friesland sheep*

## SELECTING

Choose cheese according to use and taste. Check that no mold appears on the cheese and that it has been packaged carefully.

## STORING

Wrap cheese tightly in plastic wrap or waxed paper and store it in the refrigerator. (Some cheesemakers prefer waxed paper, because plastic tends to make the cheese exude moisture.) Cheese carefully stored in a cheese section or crisper of a refrigerator will keep for about two weeks. If you will be serving the cheese within a day, store it at room temperature, covered with a cheese cloche or plastic wrap.

If mold appears on firm cheese, cut it away and use the cheese as you would normally. If mold appears on fresh or soft-ripened cheese, throw it out.

## PUTTING UP

Hard, semi-firm, and semi-soft cheeses can be frozen, but freezing will probably affect their flavor and texture. Fresh goat's or sheep's milk cheese can be preserved in good olive or vegetable oil combined with any number of flavorings. The cheeses should be used within four weeks.

## PREPARING

Cheese is best served at room temperature. Remove it from the refrigerator about two hours before serving. If the cheese is to be grated or crumbled, chill it.

## SERVING SUGGESTIONS

The best way to serve cheese is simple: A single slice of good cheese, a beautiful piece of fruit, some good bread, and a glass of wine is perfect. A plate of two or three cheeses can serve as lunch, a light dinner, or, together with fruit, as a dessert.

The uses for cheese are infinite. Cheese is delicious for breakfast, served on toast, a bagel, or a muffin, or in an omelet. Cheese can be served as an hors d'oeuvre on crackers, toast, or with vegetables or fruit. Cheeses have infinite uses in cooking, including in soups (either as cheese soup or as a garnish), casseroles, pasta sauces, as the main flavoring for breads, rolls, or crackers (cheese straws), and in desserts (cheesecake).

## TOM & NANCY CLARK

### OLD CHATHAM SHEEPHERDING COMPANY
### Columbia County • Old Chatham, New York 12136
**Stand at Union Square (Manhattan)**

One of the most successful makers of sheep's cheese in the United States is the Old Chatham Sheepherding Company, located near Chatham, New York, in Columbia County. Owner Tom Clark grew up in Dutchess County, and as a boy won a prize at the Rhinebeck fair with one of his grandfather's sheep. He vowed then and there to establish the largest sheep farm in the country. Although he became an investment banker after graduating from Cornell, he has realized his dream—and then some.

Established in 1994 with only 150 sheep, Old Chatham Farm is now the largest sheep dairy farm in the United States, with more than 1,000 dairy sheep. In addition to the cheese business, the Old Chatham Company also operates an exquisite inn and an acclaimed restaurant.

Old Chatham uses East Friesland sheep, specially bred to produce more milk than other breeds of sheep. (A sheep produces less than two quarts of milk a day, while an average cow produces about 40 quarts.) At the Old Chatham Dairy, cheese is made in a state-of-the-art creamery, using the most up-to-date methods.

Old Chatham produces a number of signature products. Among them is a fresh sheep's milk cheese (rather like chèvre), several soft-ripened cheeses, including a Peppered Pyramid that took Best of Class at the 1998 World Championship Cheese Contest. They also make a cow and sheep's milk Camembert called Hudson Valley Camembert, an Old World sheep's milk ricotta, and a sheep's milk yogurt. Cheeses from Old Chatham are served at several acclaimed New York restaurants, but the folks at Old Chatham especially enjoy coming to Greenmarket because it gives them a chance to talk to some of their New York customers.

*Cheesemaker Alison Appleby*

# CHERRIES

The expression "as American as apple pie" could easily be changed to "as American as cherry pie." Certainly few foods are more reminiscent of the Fourth of July than fresh cherries.

## VARIETIES

Cherries fall into two general categories, sweet and sour.

**SWEET CHERRIES.** Bing cherries and other varieties of sweet cherries appear at Greenmarket for about three weeks in late June and early July.

**SOUR CHERRIES.** Montmorency and other sour varieties are smaller, more delicate, and far less sweet. They are more perishable than sweet cherries. They also appear in late June for about three weeks.

## SELECTING

Choose cherries that are plump, large (to ensure sweetness), somewhat soft, dark in color (for their variety), and smooth, without blemishes. Cherries will last longer if they have not been stemmed; the stems should be green.

## STORING

Store cherries, unwashed, in a perforated plastic bag, in the refrigerator. They will keep for three to five days. Wash, stem, and pit them just before using.

## PUTTING UP

Cherries can easily, especially in syrup, for use as pie filling. Cherries freeze very well in syrup (to hold their color), or in a sugar-pack. Alternatively, cherries can simply be washed thoroughly, gently dried, stemmed, pitted, and then placed in airtight plastic containers or freezer bags and frozen. They will last for about a year.

Cherries can be pickled and preserved as jams, jellies, or juices. Cherries can also be dried, but that requires special equipment.

## PREPARING

Just before using, sort the cherries and discard any that have become too soft, withered, or have gone bad. Rinse the cherries gently under cold water; drain. Stem and pit them carefully with a cherry pitter, the tip of a vegetable peeler, or the point of a paring knife. If you don't mind if the cherry flesh becomes crushed, use your fingers.

## SERVING SUGGESTIONS

Sweet cherries can be eaten raw, used in fruit compotes, or in ice cream. They are commonly used in baked dishes such as cakes, cobblers, dessert crêpes, and, of course, pies. Poached cherries make delicious sauces for sweets such as ice cream, waffles, and pancakes, and also for meats such as chicken or duck.

Sour cherries can be too tart to eat raw, and usually require extra sweetening. Add sour cherries to compotes of sweeter fruits, ice cream, or yogurt. Sour cherries also cook well in baked goods.

---

### MARTHA STEWART'S SOUR CHERRY PIE
**Makes one 9-inch pie**

*This is a variation on a delicious recipe from Martha Stewart's Pies and Tarts.*

4   cups pitted sour cherries plus
    1 cup cherry juice
1   cup sugar
1   tablespoon all-purpose flour
2   tablespoons cornstarch
    Juice and grated zest of 1 lemon
1   9-inch unbaked pastry shell plus
    extra pastry for a lattice top
2   tablespoons cold butter, cut into
    small pieces
1   egg beaten with 2 tablespoons
    heavy cream, for a glaze

Preheat oven to 400°F. Combine the cherries and juice in a large mixing bowl and sprinkle in the sugar, flour, cornstarch, and lemon juice and zest. Toss well and pour into the pastry shell. Dot with butter and weave the lattice top over the filling. Brush the lattice and the pastry edges with the glaze and bake for about 50 minutes, until the pastry is golden. Let cool slightly and serve.

---

On the Friday after Thanksgiving, the first Christmas evergreens begin to arrive at Greenmarket and the holiday season has begun. Evergreen boughs, ropes, and arrangements are sold at many markets; Christmas trees, however, are sold primarily at Union Square and Grand Army Plaza (and occasionally at a few of the other markets). Also, many producers sell products that make fabulous holiday presents, including jams, jellies, vinegars, oils, honey, maple syrup, dried flower arrangements, knitted garments, untooled leather items, and much more. You can do virtually all of your holiday shopping at Greenmarket.

## VARIETIES

Many varieties of evergreen Christmas trees and decorations (boughs, wreaths, roping, and arrangements) are sold at Greenmarket. They fall into the categories of fir, spruce, or pine trees.

## Fir Trees

These tall, handsome trees are very fragrant, have pretty flat needles and strong branches that are good for hanging heavy ornaments.

**CANNON FIR** has short, strong needles and is fuller than Fraser, but not as full as Douglas.

**CONCOLOR FIR,** also known as white fir, looks like a blue spruce, but with longer, flatter needles and a lovely citrus smell.

**DOUGLAS FIR** is a classic Christmas tree with soft, bushy branches that are fuller than the Fraser.

**FRASER FIR** is a silvery green color with short, flat needles and strong, well-spaced branches.

## Spruce Trees

Although they resemble firs, spruce needles are round, whereas fir needles are flat. Most spruce trees have a classic Christmas tree shape and fragrance.

**BLUE SPRUCE** has a bluish cast.

**ENGELMANN SPRUCE** has finer, more elegant needles with a similar bluish cast.

## Pine Trees

Although not as fragrant as fir trees, pine trees have longer needles than most other evergreens, and many people consider them to be softer and prettier. The trees may shed needles more readily.

**EASTERN WHITE PINE** has fine, soft, especially long needles and is prettily bushy.

**RED PINE** has long, thick needles, and is robustly bushy.

**SCOTCH PINE,** one of the most common Christmas trees, has long bluish needles, reddish bark, and a rich, dense appearance.

## Decorative Evergreens

In addition to traditional Christmas trees and greens, these evergreens are available:

**HOLLY,** the classic Christmas shrub, comes in many varieties and produces evergreen boughs with lustrous, shiny, dark blue-green leaves and red, black, or purple berries. Occasionally a whole holly tree is available at Christmas time.

**JUNIPER,** a lovely shrub with soft bluish green boughs and berries, is available in bunches or potted, making a lovely miniature Christmas tree that can be kept throughout the year as a houseplant or terrace container plant, or replanted outdoors.

*Cannon fir*

*Concolor fir*

*Douglas fir*

*Fraser fir*

*Blue Spruce*

*Engelmann spruce*

*White pine*

*Red pine*

## SELECTING

Needle retention, beauty, and fragrance are what we look for in a Christmas tree. Beauty and fragrance are easy to come by and obvious. Needle retention is more difficult to foresee and is based on freshness. (As one farmer is fond of saying, you can't fool Mother Nature.)

All Christmas trees at Greenmarket are grown by the producer who is selling them, are freshly cut, and will keep, with only minor loss of needles, for several weeks. Look for trees and greens with no signs of dried needles or leaves, or, in the case of holly and juniper, shriveled berries.

## STORING

Place Christmas trees in water as soon as possible. Set up the tree in a stand that is large enough to keep the tree steady, especially after it is decorated. Water it daily.

Arrange loose evergreen boughs (pine, spruce, holly, juniper) in a large vase of water. If the boughs have thick, woody stems, scrape away the bark, split the stems up about two inches, and remove lower leaves or needles. Fresh evergreen wreaths and ropes will keep for several weeks without special care.

## DECORATING

All Christmas trees are beautiful, and you don't need boxes of heirloom ornaments to achieve a wonderful look. Lights, however, are essential and are not expensive. Be sure to wind them around the tree boughs, running them inside the tree to the trunk and then back out again. In addition to conventional ornaments, decorate with bows, fruit, candy, strung popcorn, cookies, dried flowers, children's artwork, and memorabilia.

In addition to (or instead of) a tree, decorate with a simple wreath on a door, wall, window, or used as a centerpiece; an evergreen arrangement; or roping wrapped around a door, window, fireplace, or railing. If you have a terrace or window boxes, use evergreens to decorate them as well. Combine greens with fresh or potted flowers, especially poinsettia or paperwhites.

W S S F

# JOEL PODKAMINER

TRUMANSBURG TREE FARMS • Tompkins County • Trumansburg, New York 14886

Stands at Union Square and I.S. 44 (Manhattan); Grand Army Plaza and Borough Hall (Brooklyn)

Growing Christmas trees is one of the trickiest methods of farming. Not only does it involve a risky single crop that takes years to mature (from 6 to 15, depending upon the species), but the primary selling season is a mere four weeks per year, from the day after Thanksgiving until late on Christmas Eve.

A Greenmarket veteran who grows some of the most beautiful Christmas trees available is Joel Podkaminer, the owner of the 140-acre Trumansburg Farm. Although he majored in political science at Ithaca College, Joel found his calling when he began selling Christmas trees to make extra money while going to school. Growing trees became a passion, and the work fit in with Joel's love of the outdoors. At any one time, Joel grows about 100,000 trees that are in various stages of development, from seedlings to fully mature trees. Each tree must be trimmed

at least once a year to insure that it is attractively shaped, straight, and full. During the summer, Joel employs a small crew to help out.

Joel has been coming to Greenmarket since 1982, and over the years has developed a devoted clientele who return year after year. Many New York churches and office buildings feature Joel's trees, including the World Trade Center and New York's City Hall. Each year Joel also brings a knowledgeable team of friends (especially Steven Grahling and Al Peckenpaugh), relatives (particularly his son, Jacob), and countrymen—that is, folks who love celebrating the holiday season at Greenmarket.

*Joel Podkaminer and his son Jacob*

# CIDER

Very popular in Colonial America, cider was introduced here by the English. In Colonial times, all cider was slightly alcoholic, but in recent years, cider has come to mean a "sweet" (or nonalcoholic) fruit juice, while the alcoholic variety is referred to as "hard" cider. Over the past few years, cider has enjoyed renewed popularity.

## VARIETIES

Cider is made by pressing juice from fruit, usually apples or pears.

**HARD (OR DRAFT) CIDER.** Old-fashioned fermented apple or pear juice. A fizzy, mildly alcoholic drink, the making of good cider requires the same amount of knowledge as the making of good wine.

**SWEET CIDER.** Unfermented apple or pear juice. Sweet cider is sometimes flavored with juice from other fruits, such as raspberries or grapes.

## SELECTING

Selecting the best cider is like choosing a good wine. The flavor varies according to the type of apple used and how it is processed. You have to taste-test different types to find one that suits you.

## STORING

Store sweet cider in a tightly closed jug in the refrigerator. It will keep for two weeks.

## PUTTING UP

Sweet cider can be frozen. Simply freeze it in a plastic container.

## SERVING SUGGESTIONS

As an alternative to wine, serve cider plain or with smoked salmon, seafood, cured meats, cheeses, pâtés, and spicy ethnic foods such as Mexican, Thai, or Indian. Try using cider to braise strongly flavored greens, to poach fish, and to make vinegar and sauces.

# Elizabeth Ryan

**Hudson Valley Draft Cider Company** • Dutchess County
Staatsburg, New York 12580
Stands at Union Square and I.S. 44 (Manhattan)

Elizabeth Ryan comes to the cider business naturally. For starters, she has a degree in pomology (the science of growing fruit and fruit trees) from Cornell University and sits on the advisory board of Cornell's College of Agriculture and Life Sciences. Since 1983 she has been part-owner of Breezy Hill Orchard, a 35-acre farm in Dutchess County, not far from Rhinebeck. (Elizabeth has been coming to Greenmarket since 1983, and has served on the Farmer/Consumer Advisory Board at various times.) At Breezy Hill, Elizabeth grows more than 50 varieties of apples, including many old and fascinating heirlooms.

Elizabeth has been making and selling sweet cider since she first began farming. But she also developed

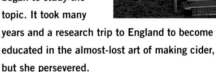

an interest in fermented ciders and began to study the topic. It took many years and a research trip to England to become educated in the almost-lost art of making cider, but she persevered.

Finally, in 1996, Elizabeth founded the Hudson Valley Draft Cider Company with Hilary Baum, daughter of famed restaurateur Joseph Baum. That year, her company introduced two draft ciders: Hudson Valley Farmhouse Cider, a bright, clean sparkling cider sold in Champagne-like bottles; and Maeve, named for a legendary Irish queen, a fragrant, dry, delicate cider. In 1998, the company introduced a fermented pear cider called Farmhouse Perry.

Elizabeth remains a committed "orchardist" and fruit specialist. She runs a good-sized farm that includes a successful pick-your-own business, farmstand, and bakery. But she has fallen in love with cider, and has launched a new endeavor that seems destined to succeed.

# COLLARD GREENS

Collards are well-known in the American South, especially as an accompaniment to barbecue or a part of "soul food" menus. Collards, with large, smooth, dark-colored leaves, are members of the large Brassica family, which also includes cabbages, kale, and broccoli. Their flavor is sort of a cross between spinach and kale. When braised, collard greens make a savory side dish that accompanies ham or pork perfectly.

## SELECTING

Look for richly colored green leaves with no sign of wilting or decay. Collards should have a mild, cabbage-like fragrance.

## STORING

Store collard greens, loose and unwashed, in the crisper of the refrigerator. Use them within three days of purchase.

## PUTTING UP

It is virtually impossible to can or dry collard greens. Like many other greens, they can be frozen in a soup or puree base; simply cook the recipe to the point where it is part of a stock or puree, then freeze it in an airtight container. The stock or puree will keep for one year.

## PREPARING

When ready to prepare the collard greens, wash them thoroughly in cool water. Like spinach, you may need to soak and rinse them several times to make sure all traces of sand have been removed. Discard wilted leaves and cut off stems or spines, which are inedible. Dry the leaves thoroughly.

For some dishes, collard greens may need to be blanched first to temper the harsh, bitter flavor; this depends on the age and thickness of the greens and the dish you are preparing.

Collards cook down considerably from their raw form. In general, 1 pound of raw collard greens produces $1/2$ cup cooked greens.

## SERVING SUGGESTIONS

In classic Southern recipes, collards are cooked very slowly with a ham hock or salt pork for as long as eight hours, then served as an accompaniment to ham, roast pork, chicken, game, barbecued dishes, and other Southern specialties.

Collard greens can be used in combination with other closely related greens, including kale, cabbage, dandelion greens, spinach, or mustard greens. They can be blanched, sautéed, or braised for use as a side dish or combined with other cooked dishes, such as omelettes, quiches, and soups. For most palates, collards are a bit harsh to use as a salad green.

### TERRIE'S COLLARDS
#### Serves 4 to 6

*This is how Terrie Mangrum, chef of the Hog Pit in Greenwich Village, prepares her collard greens.*

  3  pounds collard greens, carefully washed and trimmed
  1  ham hock or 1 thick slice of country ham
  1  medium onion, finely chopped
  1  cup white wine vinegar
  ¼  cup sugar
  2  teaspoons red pepper flakes
1½  teaspoons freshly ground black pepper
    Salt

Combine the greens, ham hock, onion, wine vinegar, sugar, pepper flakes, black pepper, salt, and enough water to cover the greens in a large stockpot and bring to a boil. Reduce to a simmer and keep the water at a gentle simmer.

Go on about your day, checking every hour or two to make sure the water has not boiled away. If it has, add a bit more to keep the greens moist. Cook for at least 8 hours. Serve hot.

# CORN

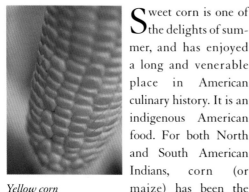

*Yellow corn*

*White corn*

Sweet corn is one of the delights of summer, and has enjoyed a long and venerable place in American culinary history. It is an indigenous American food. For both North and South American Indians, corn (or maize) has been the foundation of their diet for thousands of years.

Corn begins to appear at Greenmarket in late June, and its arrival is greeted with great excitement by urban shoppers. Corn is available until September.

## VARIETIES

More than 200 varieties of sweet corn exist, but they basically fall into three categories:

**BICOLOR CORN** is a hybrid that features both yellow and white kernels and comes in charmingly named varieties such as Peaches and Cream.

**WHITE CORN** has smaller, sweeter, white kernels; Silver Queen is the best-known and most popular variety.

**YELLOW CORN** is old-fashioned, classic corn with large, flavorful, bright yellow kernels; Early Sunglow is a well-known variety.

**A NOTE ABOUT SWEETNESS:** In recent years, many corn varieties have been developed for sweetness (Super-Sweet is one variety) or to create corn that does not lose its sweetness quickly. However, sometimes these varieties, while very sweet, lack the true, old-fashioned corn flavor.

## SELECTING

Choose ears that have bright green, grassy, snug husks and fresh-looking amber silk. The kernels should be plump and the rows tight. The stems should be green, moist, and fresh looking.

Never buy corn that has been husked; after the husk has been removed, the corn loses almost all its flavor. (Greenmarket farmers become distressed when shoppers husk corn as they choose it because they cannot sell the partially husked ears.) Run your hand gently along the husk and feel for firmness and plumpness.

Purchase corn early in the morning, and choose ears from the bottom of the piles, where the corn has stayed cooler and thus lost less of its sweetness.

## STORING

After corn is picked, its sugar immediately begins to turn to starch and, as a result, it begins to lose its flavor. Conventional wisdom holds that corn should be eaten within three hours of being picked, or, to put it more poetically, before nightfall on the day it is harvested. Thanks to Greenmarket, city dwellers can come close to meeting this goal.

Store corn, unshucked, in the refrigerator from the moment you arrive

---

### OLD-FASHIONED SUCCOTASH
#### Serves 4 to 6

*The name succotash comes from an Algonquian Indian word and it is likely that American settlers learned about the combination of corn and beans from the Indians. Some old recipes claim that it was originally made with kidney beans and seasoned with bear grease.*

  2  pounds lima beans (enough to make 2 cups of shelled beans)
1 to 6  ears of corn (enough to make 2 cups when cut off the cobs)
  2  tablespoons butter

    Salt and freshly ground pepper
  1  teaspoon sugar
  ½  cup water
  ¼  cup heavy cream

Shell the lima beans. Place them in a saucepan, cover with salted water, and cook until tender, about 20 minutes. Drain.

Shuck the corn, remove all the silk, and cut the kernels from the cobs. In a nonreactive skillet, melt the butter over medium heat. Add the corn, 1 teaspoon of salt, pepper, sugar, and ½ cup water. Simmer for about 5 minutes. Add the lima beans and the heavy cream. Warm through and serve.

---

Please! Do not husk the Corn! Others do not buy it after it has been handled. We guarantee our corn. If you get a bad ear we will replace it! Thank you. — Terry's Farm

home. If you cannot prepare the corn the day you purchase it, dip the ears, husks and all, into cold water, wrap the ears in a dish towel, and store them in the refrigerator crisper for up to two days. Alternatively, parboil the corn for about one minute, store in a plastic bag in the refrigerator, then finish boiling immediately before serving.

## PUTTING UP

Corn freezes, cans, and preserves very well by itself or in infinite combinations with other vegetables. To freeze corn, remove it from the cob, pack it in an airtight container or plastic freezer bag, and freeze. Corn on the cob can also be frozen, but won't taste nearly as delectable as fresh. To freeze it, remove the husk and silk, place the cobs in a plastic bag, and freeze.

## PREPARING

To shuck corn, tear the green leaves from the husk. To pull off the clingy silk, gently rub a paper towel down the sides of the ear. If you are serving corn on the cob, leave a bit of stem as a handle, or cut the cobs into 3- or 4-inch lengths, to make eating it a bit easier.

To remove corn kernels from the cob, slice the end off the tip to create a flat surface. Hold the ear on the flat end in a shallow dish and, using a sharp non-carbon-steel knife, slice the kernels off in a downward motion.

The preparation of corn on the cob is a topic of great controversy. One method: Place husked corn in a pot of boiling water for about 4 minutes. Some very knowledgeable cooks recommend cooking only 2 to 3 minutes, others swear by steaming the corn for as long as 5 minutes, still others recommend letting the corn rest in the water for 5 minutes. In any case, do not overcook it or add salt to the cooking water because the corn will become tough and tasteless. (You can add sugar, however, for extra sweetness.)

Corn can be roasted on a grill. Prepare it by tearing back the husks, removing the silk, moistening the husks, then rewrapping them around the corn.

## SERVING SUGGESTIONS

Corn is a staple of many cuisines throughout the world, and is made into flour, meal, oils, syrups, and whiskeys.

Fresh corn is best served steamed, on the cob, with butter and salt. However, if holding a cob in your fingers and slurping off the delicious kernels is not to your taste, remove the kernels and sauté them gently in sweet butter and milk or cream.

Fresh corn can be added to soups, stews, casseroles, puddings, stir-fries, and salads. Corn kernels add flavor and texture to corn breads and muffins made with cornmeal. Corn combines well with other vegetables, especially beans, such as in classic succotash (see page 95), and peppers, as in many Tex-Mex and Mexican dishes.

Corn husks are used for making tamales and as wrappings for other stuffed dishes.

## CORN PUDDING WITH TARRAGON
### Serves 4 to 6

*This is another old-fashioned favorite. Parsley can be substituted for the tarragon.*

3 to 6 ears of corn (enough to make 2 cups when cut off the cobs)
3 eggs, beaten
¼ cup flour
1 teaspoon salt
½ teaspoon white pepper
3 tablespoons minced fresh tarragon
2 tablespoons butter, melted
2 cups light cream or half-and-half

Preheat the oven to 325°F. Shuck the corn, remove all the silk, and slice the kernels from the cobs. Combine the corn and the eggs in a bowl. Stir in the flour, salt, pepper, and tarragon and mix thoroughly. Mix in the butter and cream.

Pour the pudding into a buttered 1½-quart baking dish or casserole and bake for about 1 hour, or until a knife inserted in the center comes out clean. Serve warm.

# CUCUMBERS

Cucumbers originated in India, and are often teamed as a cooling salad or garnish with a hot Indian curry. Their mild flavor and crispness are integral counterpoints to many spicy Mediterranean cuisines, especially Middle Eastern, Moroccan, and Greek.

## VARIETIES

Cucumbers fall into three categories:

**GREENHOUSE CUCUMBERS.** Asian and European varieties, many of which are seedless, are often grown in greenhouses.

**PICKLING CUCUMBERS.** Stubbier than the salad cukes, with a paler, bumpier skin, this variety is usually used for pickling. The kirby is the best-known variety.

**SALAD CUCUMBERS.** Also called gourmet, field, or slicing cucumbers, these are the conventional, dark green cucumbers that are commonly used for salads and other dishes.

## SELECTING

Look for cucumbers that are no longer than 8 inches (except for a few unusual varieties), with smooth, dark green skins free of bruises or brown marks. Smaller, younger cucumbers are less bitter, have thinner skins, and fewer seeds.

## STORING

Store cucumbers in the refrigerator, unwashed and unpeeled, in a plastic bag. They will keep for as long as seven days.

## PUTTING UP

The most common way to preserve cucumbers is to make pickles. Pickling is tricky; however, if you are adventurous, consult a good preserving guide. Cucumbers do not freeze or dry well.

## PREPARING

Peel mature or waxed cucumbers; younger cucumbers, with thinner, sweeter skins, can be left unpeeled. Cucumbers should be drained to ensure that they remain crisp whether or not they are to be cooked. To drain, peel the cucumbers, trim the ends, slice them in half lengthwise or in rounds, and remove the seeds. Place the cucumbers in a colander or strainer, sprinkle with salt, and let them stand for an hour to permit the salt to draw out excess water. Cucumbers can be baked, braised, sautéed, or steamed.

## SERVING SUGGESTIONS

Cucumbers, raw, can be used in crudité platters, salads, sandwiches, and as garnishes. They combine well with yogurt, cream sauces, and herbs. Cooked cucumbers make a nice side dish for fish and poultry, and can serve as the base for refreshing soups.

### CUCUMBER SALAD WITH FRESH HERBS
#### Serves 4

*Cucumber salad is often made with dill, but this one features chives, marjoram, and tarragon.*

- 2 cucumbers
- 1 tablespoon salt, preferably kosher
- 2 tablespoons cider vinegar
- 1 shallot, minced
- 1 cup sour cream
- 2 tablespoons chopped fresh chives
- 1 tablespoon chopped fresh marjoram
- 2 tablespoons chopped fresh tarragon plus 1 sprig, for garnish
- Salt and freshly ground pepper

Peel and slice the cucumbers into rounds. Sprinkle with the salt, and allow them to drain in a colander for 1 hour.

In a serving bowl, combine the vinegar and the shallot; whisk in the sour cream until smooth, then add the chives, marjoram, tarragon, and salt and pepper to taste.

Add the cucumbers and toss until the cucumbers are evenly coated. Garnish with a sprig of fresh tarragon. Chill before serving.

# EDIBLE FLOWERS

*Nasturtiums*

E dible flowers are fascinating. Some blossoms are hearty enough to be stuffed, others make colorful additions to salads, and still others serve as beautiful accents on any serving platter.

## VARIETIES

The following are among the more common edible flowers found at Greenmarket:

**FRUIT BLOSSOMS.** Blossoms from apple, peach, and plum trees that make fragrant and flavorful garnishes.

**LAVENDER.** A beautiful purple relative of the mint family that can be used in salads, teas and tisanes, and as a garnish on both savory and sweet dishes.

**MARIGOLDS.** Bright yellow flowers that are used for flavor and color in salads, soups, and for garnishing.

**NASTURTIUMS.** Colorful yellow and orange flowers that can be used whole as a garnish or minced to add

*Lavender*

vivid color and a peppery flavor to salads and sauces.

**PANSIES.** Pretty, tender flowers that come in a wide variety of colors and are used primarily for decoration.

**SQUASH BLOSSOMS.** The bright yellow or orange flowers that grow at the tips of squash fruit. They make handsome garnishes and can be stuffed and sautéed as an appetizer.

## SELECTING

Choose blossoms that are bright and fresh-looking and have not begun to wilt.

## STORING

Edible flowers are highly perishable, should be stored in water in the refrigerator, and used within 24 hours.

## PUTTING UP

The beauty of edible flowers is their delicacy and freshness. Nevertheless, they can also be preserved in vinegars, oils, or butters. In some cases, the flowers can be dried.

## PREPARING

To clean, dip the delicate blossoms in a bowl of cool water or hold under a very gentle tap and pat dry.

## SERVING SUGGESTIONS

Use edible flowers sparingly. Like certain herbs, the fragrance and flavor of some flowers, if used in excess, can overwhelm a dish. Use blossoms as a garnish on poultry or roasts, on serving platters, and on cakes. Depending on the variety, use them, whole or minced, in soups, stews, salads, and sauces, and in prepared vinegars, oils, and butters.

*Squash blossoms*

### STUFFED SQUASH BLOSSOMS
#### Serves 4 as an appetizer

*There are many recipes for stuffed squash blossoms, but this is one of the easiest.*

12 to 14  small squash blossoms
          (6 to 8 large blossoms)
    4  ounces chèvre or other soft cheese
    1  cup water
       About $\frac{1}{2}$ cup all-purpose flour
    2  cups vegetable oil, or to depth
       of about 1 inch in a skillet
       Salt

Open the flowers and remove the pistils. Form small balls with the cheese. Press 1 ball firmly into the center of each flower, then seal the petals around the cheese.

Pour the water into a shallow bowl. Sift the flour into the water, and stir until a thin batter is formed. In a skillet, heat the oil over high heat until bubbly. Coat the stuffed blossoms with the batter, then slip them into the oil. Using a spatula, cook for 3 to 4 minutes, turning 2 or 3 times, until they turn golden. Drain on paper towels, then place on a serving platter, salt to taste, and serve hot.

# EGGPLANT

*Bambino Eggplant*

Eggplant is the glamour girl (or boy—the vegetable produces both male and female fruits) of both the garden and the market. It is a breathtakingly beautiful vegetable; whether you choose the deep purple variety or the white, it is smooth, glossy, and luscious to look at as well as to eat. Although it is often associated with Italian, Greek, and other Mediterranean cuisines, eggplant was originally cultivated in India.

## SELECTING

Like zucchini, eggplant used to be judged for its size by proud American farmers. And like zucchini, eggplant had a reputation for being a rather tasteless vegetable, because the larger the eggplant, the less tasty it is. Therefore, look for the younger, smaller vegetables. Bambino (baby) eggplant are occasionally available at Greenmarket, and are a special delight.

Choose eggplants that are firm and heavy for their size. The skin should be smooth, even in color, and without any brown spots. Go for the female fruit—that is, the one with the indented stem end.

## STORING

Eggplant, despite it robust appearance, is quite perishable and loses its flavor, becomes bitter, and rots quickly. If you are going to use it within a day or two, store it in a cool, dry place. It can also be stored in a plastic bag in the refrigerator for up to five days.

## PUTTING UP

Because eggplant is so fragile and porous, it does not freeze or can attractively. Preserved caponata relish is the best bet.

## PREPARING

Many recipes call for eggplant to be peeled, but peeling is not necessary if the eggplant is young and fresh. Because eggplant can be bitter, recipes often call for the slices to be sprinkled with salt and weighted to extract extra moisture and any bitterness. Also, because eggplant is very porous, it absorbs oil easily, so care must be taken when cooking it.

## SERVING SUGGESTIONS

Eggplant is a mild-flavored, meaty vegetable that absorbs stronger flavors—olive oil, onions, tomatoes, and herbs, for example—extremely well. Therefore it can be used as a base for any number of dishes. It can be stuffed with vegetables or meat, or used in casseroles or pasta sauces.

Three dishes have made eggplant famous: eggplant Parmigiana, moussaka (an eggplant-based Greek casserole), and ratatouille (a vegetable mélange of tomatoes, peppers, zucchini, and eggplant). Perhaps less well-known is caponata, a vegetable mixture that can be served as a cold hors d'oeuvre or a relish with roasts.

Eggplant can be served as a side dish, prepared in a number of ways: deep-fried, sautéed with herbs in olive oil, broiled, or grilled over charcoal.

*White and dark-purple eggplant*

# EGGS

Eggs, like milk, are a near-perfect food. Despite controversy over the cholesterol in egg yolks, eggs remain a staple.

## VARIETIES

CHICKEN EGGS. Most commonly used for eating and baking. Eggs are ranked by weight (peewee, small, medium, large, extra-large, and jumbo); large eggs are the best bet for most uses.

GAME BIRD EGGS. Some farmers offer eggs from turkeys, ducks, quail, and other game birds. These have stronger flavors.

## SELECTING

All eggs sold at Greenmarket are very fresh and are sold in conventional egg cartons. Check that none are cracked.

## STORING

Store eggs in the carton in which you bought them in the refrigerator. Eggs tend to absorb odors, so store them away from foods with strong odors. Eggs will keep for about four weeks in the refrigerator.

## PUTTING UP

Separated eggs can be frozen. Place egg whites in an airtight container and freeze. Place yolks in an airtight container, add $\frac{1}{8}$ teaspoon salt, and freeze. Frozen eggs will keep for six months. Use eggs that have been frozen only in foods with long cooking times, such as baked goods and puddings.

## PREPARING AND SERVING

To avoid possible salmonella poisoning, avoid dishes that call for raw eggs. Eggs can be soft-boiled, hard-boiled, poached, fried, or scrambled. They can be prepared as omelettes, soufflés, and frittatas, and are integral to baked goods and many sauces.

W S S F

# BOB & ALICE MESSERICH

KNOLL KREST FARM • Dutchess County • Clinton Corners, New York 12514
Stand at Union Square (Manhattan)

**B**ob and Alice Messerich have a small, unassuming egg stand at the Union Square Greenmarket, but when you see the long lines coming from the Messeriches's area, you know they are selling something extraordinary. And they are!

What makes Messerich eggs and chickens so special? First, Bob and Alice are selling the freshest eggs and chickens possible. What's more, their birds eat only natural grains and are not subject to hormones, antibiotics, or other artificial substances. (Messerich eggs are also carefully tested to be sure they contain no salmonella.)

Knoll Krest Farm was started by Anthony Messerich, Bob's dad, in 1946. Bob was one of three sons, and before taking over the family business, he served in the armed services and studied journalism at Syracuse University. Bob took over Knoll Krest in 1953, running it solely as an egg business for years. (In fact, Knoll Krest Farm is the only egg farm remaining in Dutchess Country.) However, a few years ago, Bob realized he needed to diversify and begin selling directly to consumers.

Today, the Messeriches actually have two farms, one specializing in laying hens (eggs), the other for raising birds for meat. These days, Alice makes the selling trips to New York. As with most Greenmarket farmers, market days are tough and long, but worth it. Not only does Greenmarket provide Bob and Alice with a strong market for their eggs and meat, but it gives them one-on-one contact with many very appreciative consumers.

# FIDDLEHEAD FERNS

Fiddlehead ferns, the green shoots of the ostrich fern, are picked before the leaves unfurl. Along with ramps (see page 212), it is one of two great spring delicacies offered at Greenmarket. The term "fiddlehead" refers to the tightly curled baby fern, which resembles the shape of a violin or fiddle. Fiddleheads are a delightful sign that spring has arrived, and a tasty accompaniment to many dishes, especially lamb. They are sometimes compared to asparagus in flavor, but given their chewy texture, they can also taste a bit like okra.

## SELECTING

At Greenmarket, fiddlehead ferns begin to appear in late April or early May, and are available for only about three weeks. Choose small, deep green, tightly coiled ferns.

## STORING

Fiddlehead ferns are highly perishable. Store, unwashed, in a plastic bag in the refrigerator, and use them within 24 hours.

## PUTTING UP

Like most tender greens, fiddlehead ferns cannot be frozen, canned, or dried. In fact, they are much more perishable than most greens.

## PREPARING

Sometimes fiddlehead ferns form a brown coating; simply rub it off. In any case, ferns should be washed carefully and thoroughly in cool water. If necessary, trim the ends. Fiddlehead ferns can be steamed, simmered, sautéed, or briefly blanched and then served chilled.

## SERVING SUGGESTIONS

Fiddlehead ferns, gently steamed and served with a light vinaigrette sauce, make a nice first course. They also make an interesting side dish, lightly buttered or gently sautéed. They go well with poultry, fish, or shellfish, and make an attractive and flavorful addition to stir-fries. Cooked or raw, fiddleheads can also be used in salads, and combine especially well with citrus fruits, mushrooms, nuts, and seeds.

### ANDREA'S FIDDLEHEAD & RAMP PASTA
#### Serves 2 as a main dish

*Photographer Andrea Sperling is a terrific cook. Here's one of her creations.*

- 1 basket (about 2 cups) fiddleheads
- 2 cloves garlic, minced
- 2 tablespoons olive oil
- 2 plum tomatoes, chopped
- 1 bunch ramps, chopped, keeping white and green parts separate
- 4 anchovies, sliced
  Red pepper flakes, to taste
  Salt and freshly ground pepper
- 1 pound wheel-shaped pasta, cooked al dente and drained
  Freshly grated Romano cheese

Wash the fiddleheads under cool water several times. In a pot, blanch the fiddleheads for 2 minutes; drain. In a skillet, sauté the garlic in olive oil until it is transparent; add the fiddleheads, the tomatoes, the white part of ramps, and the anchovies. Sauté for 5 minutes, then add the green ramp leaves and sauté for 1 minute more. Add red pepper flakes, salt and pepper to taste, and toss with the pasta. Serve with grated cheese.

# FISH & SEAFOOD

Over a half-dozen fishermen sell their catches at Greenmarket. Greenmarket fishers are subject to a similar set of grow-your-own policies that the produce growers must follow. All fish harvesters are required to sell either the fish they catch or those of local harvesters, and all fish must be caught in regional waters. Like vegetable and fruit crops, fish varieties are available seasonally. In other words, some varieties of fish are not always available in the market, as a day's catch depends on the presence of fish in the waters. Therefore, be open and creative when you shop for fish.

## VARIETIES

Scores of fish varieties are available at Greenmarket at different times of the year.

**FILLETS AND WHOLE FISH.** Flounder, fluke, mackerel, bluefish, cod, porgy, scrod, sea trout, sea bass, swordfish, tilefish, tuna, weakfish, and whiting, among others, are available as fillets, steaks, and, when appropriate, as whole fish.

**SHELLFISH.** Shellfish sold at Greenmarket includes clams (which are available year-round), lobsters, mussels (also available year-round), scallops, and occasionally squid.

**PREPARED FISH PRODUCTS.** Several fishermen sell delicious prepared fish products, including fish soups and chowders, clam sauces, dips, fish loaves or cakes, and other delicacies.

## SELECTING

Both fish and shellfish should look and smell fresh (like the sea) and have firm, unblemished flesh. The surface of the fish should be bright, clear, reflective, and almost translucent. The color should be consistent with the type of fish, such as pearly white for white fish or bright pink for red snapper. No inappropriate red, gray, or brown spots should be visible. Fish should be

firm and elastic. Gills should be bright or pink, and eyes should be bright, clear, and full. Get to know the various fishmongers and don't be afraid to ask questions.

## Storing

Most Greenmarket fish will have been frozen or iced from shortly after the catch until they reach the market. Since most home refrigerators do not get cold enough to keep the fish fresh-tasting, it is best to keep fish on ice (in a vegetable bin, baking dish, or between ice packs) even when it is in the refrigerator. Store fish in the bottom of the refrigerator where it is usually the coldest. Never store ungutted fish. Wrap fish in plastic wrap so its smell does not contaminate other food. Fish should keep for 3 to 5 days.

## Putting Up

Whole fish and fish fillets can be frozen, but only if they are very fresh, which they should be at Greenmarket. Wrap fish in two or three layers of plastic wrap and freeze. It will keep for about six months.

## Preparing

Depending upon the variety of fish, preparation (including removing scales, filleting, and combining flavors well) can be complicated. Consult a good fish cookbook for details. Fish and/or shellfish, depending upon the type, can be baked, fried, stir-fried, grilled, broiled, poached, steamed, stewed, or smoked.

## Serving Suggestions

Most fresh fish are best prepared simply, with a touch of lemon or lime juice, salt, pepper, and perhaps a light sprinkling of fresh herbs, especially tarragon, lemon thyme, or parsley. Of course, thousands of recipes have been published for ways to cook just about any fish or shellfish.

If you have leftover fish or shellfish, use it the next day to make fish soup, chowder, stew, or a cold fish salad, such as salmon or tuna salad.

# FLORENCE FENNEL

Florence fennel (also called *finoccio,* its Italian name, or sweet fennel) is a very pretty vegetable with a distinctive white bulb and a unique licorice-like flavor. It works double-time, because its succulent bulb serves as a vegetable while its feathery leaves can be used as an herb.

## SELECTING
Look for fennel with firm, clean bulbs, straight stalks, and fresh green leaves. Stalks should be tightly packed. Avoid fennel with brown spots or dried-out areas.

## STORING
Store the stalks and bulb separately in plastic bags in the refrigerator. Use the stalks within two days, the bulb within three or four days.

## PUTTING UP
Fennel is a delicate, watery vegetable, so it will not can, freeze, or dry particularly well. Its whispy leaves can be dried as you would an herb and used as a flavoring, especially as a substitute for dill.

## PREPARING
Separate the stalks from the bulb. Use the stalks in soups and sauces and for flavoring; for eating raw or cooking, slice, chop, or dice the bulb. Fennel can be baked, braised, sautéed, or steamed.

## BRAISED FENNEL
## WITH PARMESAN
### Serves 4

*The licorice flavor of fennel combines beautifully with Parmesan cheese.*

2   tablespoons olive oil
3   pounds fennel (about 2 heads), trimmed and quartered lengthwise
2½  cups chicken stock or broth
1   tablespoon chopped fresh thyme (2 teaspoons dried)
    Salt and freshly ground pepper
½   cup freshly grated Parmesan cheese

Heat the olive oil in a large skillet over medium-high heat, add the fennel, and sauté, turning frequently for about 5 minutes.

Add the chicken broth and the thyme, cover, and simmer gently over low heat for about 30 minutes, or until the fennel is very tender. The liquid should by syrupy, but if it is not, remove the fennel, bring the liquid to a boil, and cook until it becomes syrupy.

Place the fennel in a shallow baking dish and pour the sauce over it. Season with salt and pepper to taste, and sprinkle with the cheese. Bake in a preheated 375°F oven for about 15 minutes, or until the fennel is heated through and the cheese has melted and is beginning to brown.

## SERVING SUGGESTIONS

Florence fennel slices make an interesting addition to crudité platters. Fennel is delicious braised or baked as a side dish; it combines especially well with fish.

In general, fennel can be used much the same way you would use celery, although it is much more strongly flavored than celery. Use it to add a crunchy texture and flavor to casseroles, stuffings for chicken or game birds, soups, stews, and salads.

*St. George Greenmarket, Staten Island*

Photo © Simon Benepe

# FLOWERS

*A perfect Dahlia*

Flowers are available year-round at Greenmarket. From the first hyacinth in spring to the poinsettias at Christmas, flowers dress up the market beautifully.

Flower and plant growers operate under special rulings. They must be properly licensed or listed with their state Cooperative Extension. They must own their own greenhouses or else receive special permission to use another grower's greenhouses. The potted plants and flowers must be started by the farmer himself from seeds, cell packs, bulbs, cuttings, or other approved methods.

All wildflowers and some wild greens can be sold. Nevertheless, lilacs, forsythia, fruit-tree branches, and certain greens are not considered forageable and must be collected from the grower's own property or from leased property within 20 miles of his land.

## VARIETIES

A vast number of flower varieties are available at Greenmarket in various forms, including freshly cut, potted, or in seedling flats. Here are a just a few:

### Cut Flowers & Greens

**ANEMONE.** A cup-shaped flower that comes in many vivid colors, including white, purple, and red. Available in spring and summer.

**COSMOS.** A delicate member of the aster family, with feathery foliage and single or double blossoms, that comes in a variety of colors, from white and lilac to scarlet. Available in late summer and fall.

**DAHLIA.** Any of a large genus of perennials that are treated as annuals. Flowers commonly known as dahlias are large, decorative pompons that come in a wide range of colors and multicolors. Available late summer and early fall.

**DAISY.** The common name for numerous members of the aster and daisy families. This group includes the Shasta daisy, white daisy, and yellow daisy, which is also known as black-eyed Susan. Available throughout the summer.

**EVERLASTING.** Any of a number of flowers that are used in permanent winter bouquets because they retain their form and color when dried. Most everlastings belong to the aster family, have ray florets, and come in delicate colors. Available year-round, either fresh or dried.

**HYDRANGEA.** A shrub that produces large, showy, ball-shaped flowers that come in electric-blue, purple, pink, and white. The flowers are sold both fresh and dried at Greenmarket. The flowers can also be dried easily at home.

**PEONY.** A perennial with long, dark green stems and huge, round pompon flowers in colors from maroon to red, pink, and white. Available in summer.

**ROSE.** The rose comes in many varieties and colors: red, pink, salmon, yellow, cream, white. At Greenmarket, roses are available in pots (bushes), hanging baskets, and as cut flowers, in both miniature and traditional sizes. Available year-round.

**SUNFLOWER.** The common name for helianthus, which is typically a tall plant with a large, heavy, daisy-like flower head. Miniature sunflowers are also available in late summer through the fall.

**WILDFLOWER.** Many wildflowers are available, including bloodroot, goldenrod, Queen Anne's lace; also wild grasses. Available from spring into the fall.

**ZINNIA.** A showy annual with bright heads that come in a broad range of colors, from magenta, shocking pink, and white to yellow, gold, and orange. A favorite old-fashioned garden flower.

## Potted Flowers & Bulbs

Potted plants, including flowering shrubs and bushes, as well as flowers grown from bulbs and seeds, are available.

**AZALEAS.** A group of shrubs belonging to the rhododendron family that come in vivid colors ranging from red, pink, and lavender to salmon, orange, yellow, and white. They come in pots and can be grown in containers indoors or out. Available from April through July.

**CHRYSANTHEMUMS.** Members of the aster family and often simply called mums, these plants have bright yellow, maroon, and white pompon flowers in various sizes, and rather coarse leaves. Available in late summer and fall.

**EASTER LILY.** A tall, white, statuesque lily that is grown from a bulb and forced to bloom at Easter. The Easter lily is closely related to other lilies that come in a range of colors. Available in spring.

**GERANIUM.** A name that is applied to several unrelated plants, the most common being the pelargonium, which has bright, pompon-like flowers that range in color from magenta and pink to white. Some geraniums come in hanging baskets. Available late spring through summer.

**GRASSES & GREENS.** Includes many cultivated grasses and greens, such as eucalyptus, that can be used alone or as part of flower arrangements. Many are available year-round, depending on the type.

**HYACINTH.** A bulb that flowers in early spring, producing a multiblossomed flower head in blue, lavender, pink, and white.

**NARCISSI.** Various trumpet-shaped flowers grown from bulbs, the daffodil being among the most common. Most narcissi are yellow or a combination of yellow and white or yellow and orange. Available in spring.

**PAPERWHITE.** Members of the narcissus family, with small, trumpet-shaped fragrant flowers perched on long, elegant stems. They are often forced to bloom during the Christmas season.

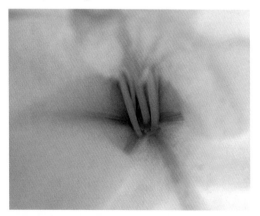

**POINSETTIA.** The common name for a tropical herb that is almost always grown as a potted plant. Available at Christmas.

**TULIPS.** Classic cup-shaped flowers, grown from bulbs, that come in an infinite range of colors, shapes, and varieties. Available, both potted and cut, in spring.

## Seedling Flats

Flats of seedlings can be purchased for use in window boxes, hanging baskets, containers (indoors or out), or gardens.

**NASTURTIUMS.** Delicate annuals that comes in bright shades of red, orange, yellow, gold, salmon, and pink. Available in late spring and summer.

**PANSIES.** Perennials grown as annuals with flat, very delicate flowers that come in a wide range of colors, from red and purple to yellow and multicolored. Available in spring.

**PETUNIAS.** Trumpet-shaped flowers that come in many shapes, sizes, and colors, including striped and ruffled flowers. Available in spring.

## SELECTING

Buy cut flowers first thing in the morning. Select flowers and plants with

*Poinsettia*

perky-looking blossoms and leaves, good color for their variety, and no sign of discoloration, tears, holes, or unsightly forms. (If you plan to dry your flowers, take special care to select perfect plants.)

## PREPARATION AND CARE

**CUT FLOWERS.** Prepare cut flowers as soon as possible. Remove lower leaves. Using sharp shears, cut each stem on a long angle to allow plenty of water to enter the stem. Plunge the blooms into clean, cool water, and store in a cool, dark place for a couple of hours. Each day, shorten stems by about one inch and change the water. Flowers, depending upon variety, can last up to five days.

*Peony*

*Rose*

*Gladiola*

**POTTED FLOWERS.** Position the pot where the plant will get sufficient light and be protected from extreme heat or cold. Water potted flowers about twice a week, depending on the variety.

**SEEDLING FLATS.** Repot plants as you would any house or garden plant.

## DRYING FLOWERS

Air-drying is the easiest method for drying flowers. To air-dry, remove excess foliage, secure the bouquets with string or a rubber band, and hang the bunches upside down in a dark, dry, well-ventilated space. Most flowers will dry in 7 to 14 days.

Flowers can also be dried using desiccants or silica gel, which draw the moisture from the plant. These methods involve complex techniques. Consult a good guide.

## DISPLAYING

Arranging different colors, shapes, and varieties of flowers artfully takes a practiced eye, talent, and skill. One simple tip: Combine in a large bouquet a single variety of flower—sunflowers, dahlias, zinnias, Queen Anne's lace, roses—whatever happens to suit your fancy or be available that day at the market. The effect is always satisfying and dramatic. Along the same lines, buy at least three pots of the same variety of potted plant—paperwhites, poinsettia, Easter lilies—and cluster them together as an arrangement.

Many flowers available at Greenmarket, especially potted flowers, shrubs, bushes, and seedlings, can be used in containers (on terraces and indoors), in window boxes, and in garden borders.

W S S F

# WALTER & BERNADETTE KOWALSKI

THE RIVER GARDEN • Greene County • Catskill, New York 12414
Stands at Union Square, World Trade Center, and Verdi Square (Manhattan)

Many romances have blossomed at Greenmarket, but none seems quite as romantic as the marriage of Bernadette Bulich and Walter Kowalski.

Bernadette is the daughter of Frank Bulich, the owner of Bulich Farms and famed for his exquisite mushrooms. For years, Bernadette, together with her eight brothers and sisters, often worked the Bulich stand at the Union Square Greenmarket. About seven years ago, Walter Kowalski began appearing at the stand next door.

Walter, who comes from Chesterfield, New Jersey, was working for Jim Durr, a Jersey flower grower and another Greenmarket regular. Walt began borrowing the Bulich broom to tidy up the Durr stand and would repay the loan with a bouquet of flowers. It soon became clear to the Bulich siblings that the flowers were meant particularly for Bernadette—and were not necessarily a thank-you for the use of the broom. Walt and Bernadette began dating and ultimately married.

Initially, neither Bernadette nor Walt had considered farming as a career. Bernadette, although she had grown up on a farm, had gone to art school intending to become an illustrator. Walter had been raised in a typical suburban town, and had seriously pursued becoming a pharmacist or a professional scuba diver. Nevertheless, by the time they married six years ago, they had decided to rent some land from Bernadette's father and see if they could make a go of the flower-growing business. As Walt says, "We had no idea what we were getting into; we just jumped in, made a lot of errors, and figured it out along the way."

Despite 14-hour work days, six or seven days a week, Bernadette and Walt have flourished. Like many small growers, they recognize that their business relies on direct selling to consumers.

# GARLIC

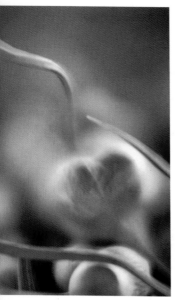

Garlic is one of the most popular flavorings in our multiethnic culture. Often, it is the fragrance that starts your mouth watering upon entering a down-to-earth French or Italian restaurant, or the kitchen of a good cook.

## VARIETIES

Garlic comes in many varieties. Among those available at Greenmarket:

**AMERICAN GARLIC.** A white, relatively strong-flavored garlic; the most common culinary garlic.

**GREEN GARLIC,** or baby garlic. Has a long, green, chive-like top and a tiny, mild-flavored bulb.

**ROCAMBOLE.** A larger garlic with a delicate, rather peppery flavor.

## SELECTING

Select firm, plump bulbs that are heavy for their size with dry skins. Avoid heads with shriveled bulbs or green shoots.

## STORING

Store garlic, unpeeled, in an open container in a cool, dark place, away from other foods, since garlic emits gases that will contaminate foods stored nearby. Garlic will keep for about two months.

## PUTTING UP

Garlic can be preserved in olive oil or wine vinegar. To prepare, peel several garlic cloves, place them in a jar, and cover with olive oil or vinegar. Close tightly and refrigerate. Beware, however: Garlic in oil can become toxic if it is not refrigerated, and garlic vinegar can become too harsh. Freezing raw garlic is not recommended; when frozen, garlic can turn acrid-tasting.

## PREPARING

For most dishes, the papery skins on the cloves must be removed. To do this, rub the cloves with your fingers, or, when working with many cloves, parboil them or heat them for one minute in the microwave oven, then slip off the skins.

Garlic cloves can be minced with a garlic press or a chef's knife. With a garlic press, place the whole clove in the press, squeeze, and discard the skin. (Wash the press thoroughly and store it open so it does not become rancid.) To mince with a knife, remove the skins, smash the cloves with the flat side of a chef's knife, then mince.

To create a buttery spread, roast a large garlic bulb (Rocambole is perfect!) in a 325°F oven for about 30 minutes. Spread the soft, warm cloves on bread or crackers.

## SERVING SUGGESTIONS

Garlic is used as a subtle flavoring in an infinite number of recipes for soups, sauces, stews, casseroles, salad dressings, and many other dishes. It is also a primary ingredient in many recipes, including aioli, garlic butter, and garlic bread.

### NO-FAIL AIOLI
**Makes about 2 cups**

*Aioli, a French garlic mayonnaise, is classically added to bourride or is served as a sauce with vegetables and fish.*

| | |
|---|---|
| 1 | slice day-old white bread, crusts removed |
| 3 | tablespoons lemon juice |
| 6 to 8 | large garlic cloves, peeled and chopped |
| 4 | egg yolks |
| 1½ | cups mild olive oil |
| | Salt and white pepper |

Place the bread in the bowl of a blender and blend until the bread is crumbled. Add the lemon juice and chopped garlic and blend at high speed until it forms a smooth paste. Add the egg yolks and blend at high speed until the mixture becomes thick and smooth.

With machine running, begin adding the oil slowly in droplets. After a third of the oil has been added, add the remaining oil in a stream. (If the mixture becomes too thick, add 2 or 3 tablespoons of boiling water.) Season with salt and pepper to taste. Serve at room temperature with a platter of vegetables.

# GRAPES

New York State has been one of the major grape-growing regions in the United States since Colonial times. Scores of varieties of grapes are grown in our region, and several of those are sold at Greenmarket. In addition to the fruit, grape juice and wine are sold.

## VARIETIES

Grapes fall into two general categories: wine grapes and table grapes. Wine grapes (cabernet, chardonnay, etc.) do not tend to be good for eating. Conversely, table grapes (Concord, Thompson seedless, etc.) do not make good wine.

Beyond this general division, grapes are categorized as American or European (both types are grown in the United States)

and seeded or unseeded. Grapes with seeds are thought to have more flavor.

Many grape varieties are sold at Greenmarket, including small quantities of Delaware, Catawba, Canadise, Marquis, Red Globe, and Vanessa grapes. Among the more common varieties sold are:

CONCORD. A major American variety. Large, round, blue-black succulent grapes with a white "bloom," sweet-tart flavor, perfumy fragrance. Perhaps the first grape discovered in North America, it is commonly used in grape preserves and juice.

NIAGARA. Large, amber-colored grapes with a grayish bloom. Either round or egg-shaped. Coarse-fleshed; less sweet, but tasty, juicy. An excellent table grape (although it is sometimes used in wine).

CHAMPAGNE GRAPES (BLACK CORINTH). Small, elegant, dark purple grapes that are very sweet and winey. In recent years, champagne grapes, a European variety, have shown up with greater frequency at several Greenmarkets.

## Grape juice

Grape juice is made by crushing grapes. If the juice is purple, it is because the skins of purple grapes have been included in the process. Some grape juices are pale green. Concord grapes are the best juicing grape. High-sugar-content grape juice has more calories, but is among the sweetest juices. Combine grape juice with lemon or grapefruit juice to add tartness to the sweet flavor.

## Wine

Wine is the fermented juice of grapes, and is one of the oldest beverages known to civilized man. Upstate New York has long been an important wine producing region. Although, perhaps, California wines enjoy greater prestige, many New York State wines hold their own, and several are sold at Greenmarket.

## SELECTING

Grapes should be picked ripe, as they will not continue to ripen after picking. Green grapes (also called white grapes) should be more translucent and yellow-green rather than opaque and dark green; all red grapes should be crimson; blue grapes should be dark—almost black.

Choose plump, succulent-looking grapes with a silvery bloom. They should have moist, flexible stems firmly attached to the fruit. Avoid wrinkled, sticky, or discolored grapes or ones with withered, brown, or brittle stems.

## STORING

Remove any spoiled grapes before storing the bunch. Place them, unwashed, in a plastic bag and store them in the refrigerator. They will keep for at least seven days.

## PUTTING UP

Grapes can be canned whole and as juice, are commonly preserved as jellies and jams, and can be frozen easily. To freeze, pull the grapes from their stems, place them on a plate or tray, and freeze. Eat frozen grapes as a snack or hold them for up to a year. Certain varieties (Concord, for example) can be held in a root cellar, but should be stored apart because they tend to absorb flavors of other foods. Dried grapes are raisins, although grape varieties grown in this region are not particularly good for drying.

## PREPARING

Wash grapes under cool water just before serving and remove any damaged or unattractive fruit. Leave the bunch whole or divide it into smaller branches, depending upon need. If the recipe asks for peeled grapes, use American grapes (Concords, Niagaras, Delawares, etc.) because the skins slide off easily.

## SERVING SUGGESTIONS

Grapes are a popular, easy-to-consume, low-calorie snack to be eaten out of hand. (In summer, they are especially refreshing after they have been frozen.) Grapes combine beautifully with other fruits and with cheese as an appetizer or dessert. They should be served just a bit cooler than room temperature, not right from the refrigerator.

Grapes are the distinguishing ingredient in sole or chicken Véronique, and add sweetness and an interesting texture to chicken, shrimp, and turkey salads, green salads, cold pasta salads, and, of course, fruit salads.

*Concord grapes*

---

### GRAPE GRANITA
#### Serves 6

*This refreshing dessert can be made in just a few minutes with Greenmarket grape juice.*

3 cups water
1½ cups sugar
2 cups grape juice
¾ cup orange juice
Juice of 2 lemons

Bring the water to a boil, and stir in the sugar until it is dissolved. Cool, then add the juices. Freeze in 3 or 4 ice cube trays or in a shallow bowl. Serve ice cold and slushy with cookies.

---

# JOHN & ANN MARTINI

ANTHONY ROAD WINE COMPANY • Seneca County
Pen Yan, New York 14527
Stand at Union Square (Manhattan)

For over 25 years, John and Ann Martini have been growing world-class grapes on the western shore of Seneca Lake in the center of New York State. The Martinis specialized in wine grapes rather than table grapes, and supplied many of New York State's larger wine makers, including Taylor. In 1989, the Martinis combined their grape-growing knowledge with the expertise of wine maker Derek Wilber and his wife, Donna. Concentrating on white wines, they produced 2,000 cases during their first year. Thus, the Anthony Road Wine Company was born.

Anthony Road Wine Company is one of 21 small wineries that are thriving along the shores of Seneca Lake in the Finger Lakes region of New York. The geological history of the Finger Lakes region makes it an ideal area for growing grapes, and vineyards have flourished on these temperate slopes since the mid-1800s. Over the years, a wide range of grape varieties have been planted and nurtured, giving the Seneca Lake region an extraordinary diversity of wines, especially whites.

The Anthony Road Wine Company specializes in Vignoles, and its Late-Harvest Vignoles have won many awards, both nationally and internationally. The company has also expanded its production to include Cabernet Franc, Chardonnay, Riesling, and Seyval wines.

For the past few years, John Martini has been making the more-than-six-hour trip to sell his wines at the Union Square Greenmarket. He enjoys the conversations with discerning New York City buyers, and welcomes the chance to introduce his wines to a wider audience.

# GREENS, COMMON & UNCOMMON

Scores of greens (not counting the lettuces) are available at Greenmarket from May through November. In addition to the familiar ones like collards and kale, many unusual greens also show up frequently. Some are cooking greens (like mustard greens or broccoli rabe), others are salad greens (like lemongrass or mizuna), while still others (like sorrel) can be cooked or served raw.

## VARIETIES

Every year, several new varieties of greens appear at Greenmarket. Here are notes on several favorites:

**ARUGULA.** Technically an herb known as rocket, arugula became very popular as a salad green. It has a relatively strong, peppery flavor, combines well with other greens, and is used frequently as the green (together with red radicchio and white Belgian endive) in an Italian *tricolore* salad. Microarugula, which is the delectable, ten-

der, baby arugula, is sometimes available at Greenmarket.

**BEET GREENS.** The leaves that grow above ground, attached to the garden-variety beet, are particularly delicious when they are young and cooked together with young, marble-sized baby beets. Mature beet greens are also tasty when sautéed as a side dish or combined with other greens in a salad, cooked side dish, or stir-fry.

**BROCCOLI RABE.** A member of the Italian branch of the broccoli family, broccoli rabe has thin stems, green leaves, and small yellow florets. It has a strong, slightly bitter flavor and sometimes benefits from blanching for a few minutes before being sautéed.

**CHICORY.** A member of the endive family, chicory has long, ragged-edged, dark green leaves that can be bitter; the inner leaves are sweeter, especially in salads. The hearty flavor and texture of chicory combine well with pork, bacon, and cheese.

**CHRYSANTHEMUM GREENS.** The leaves of the Asian relative of the chrysanthemum flower, they are medium green, spiky-shaped, and slightly bitter tasting. They add interesting flavor and texture to salads.

**DANDELION GREENS.** Leaves from a cultivated relative of the common lawn weed, which is a member of the sunflower family, they are long and dark green with saw-toothed edges, and are more tender and less bitter than the wild field greens. They taste similar to chicory, and work well in salads and cooked dishes, especially when combined with milder greens such as spinach or various lettuces.

**ESCAROLE.** A member of the chicory family, like chicory and frisée, escarole has pale green, broad leaves that are milder than their relations, but still quite flavorful. Escarole is particularly tasty in soups.

**KALE.** A member of the cabbage family,

kale resembles collard greens except that its leaves are smaller, curly rather than smooth, coarser in texture, and with a stronger flavor. Although it is most commonly green, kale comes in a variety of other colors, from red and purple to yellowish, which is sometimes called salad savoy.

**MESCLUN.** A combination of baby greens from a number of different lettuces and greens, mesclun may also include edible flowers.

**MIBUNA.** A mild-flavored, Asian green with long, oval-shaped leaves. It can be used as a salad green or cooked like spinach.

**MIZUNA.** A delicate, wispy Japanese green with a mild, appealing flavor and crisp texture. It combines well with other greens, especially in tossed salads, and is a common component in mesclun.

**MUSTARD GREENS.** Mustard greens are members of the cabbage family (like collard greens and kale). The leaves are pale green and slightly ruffled. They are more delicate than kale or collards, but still have a more pungent, peppery flavor. Occasionally, some farmers offer Asian mustard greens, which are milder than the Western variety.

**NASTURTIUM LEAVES.** The pretty, round leaves of the nasturtium flower have a peppery bite, and are sometimes compared to—and can be substituted for—watercress. They can be used in salads or as a leafy green in a sandwich.

*Mesclun*

*Mizuna*

*Mustard greens*

*Nasturtium flowers and leaves*

*Purslane*

*Radicchio*

**PURSLANE.** A trailing weed (that is, not commonly cultivated) with pretty, relatively meaty leaves that add an interesting bite and texture to salads.

**RADICCHIO.** A relative of the chicory family, with red leaves and a strong, interesting flavor. It is most commonly used in salads, and is the red leaf in a classic Italian *tricolore* salad.

**RADISH GREENS.** The tops of any variety of radish. They have a strong, biting flavor, and are commonly used in stir-fries.

**SHISO.** A cousin of mint and basil, this feathery, jagged-edged green is commonly used as a garnish in Japanese dishes. It also makes a nice salad green.

**SORREL.** An herb with leaves that closely resemble baby spinach in shape and color. It has a strong, delicious, lemony flavor, and is a classic flavoring in French sauces and soups. It is also a nice addition to green salads, particularly spinach salad.

**SPINACH.** A common green with dark green, flat leaves. For details, see page 218.

**SWISS CHARD (OR CHARD).** A relative of the beet family (without the root) with large, theatrical leaves. Cooking with Swiss chard takes finesse; its leaves are not as delicate as lettuce or spinach so a salad made solely of chard is too rough, while conversely, chard leaves steam and sauté well, but their mild flavor requires strong, thoughtful seasoning.

**TATSOI.** A Chinese green with the appearance and texture of spinach, and a fla-

vor similar to mustard greens. It makes an excellent addition to stir-fries or as a flavoring for fish.

**TURNIP GREENS.** The leaves of the turnip root are tastiest when young. They are delicious on their own, sautéed like collard or mustard greens, and add color, texture, and flavor when added to turnip dishes such as mashed turnips or cream of turnip soup.

**WATERCRESS.** A member of the mustard family, watercress literally grows in

stream beds. It has dark green leaves and a sharp flavor. It is delicious served in salads or a sandwich.

## SELECTING

Look for bright colors, no sign of wilting or decay, and a definitive fragrance, such as a light lemony smell in sorrel. If you will be cooking the greens, remember that each pound of raw greens, depending upon the variety, yields about a half cup of cooked.

## STORING

Remove any bands that might bruise the greens and discard any tired outer leaves. Store, unwashed and loose, in the refrigerator crisper. Layer and wrap damp greens in paper towels or a dish towel. (Storing fragile greens in a plastic bag, which retains moisture, makes them turn limp quickly.) Greens stay fresh and crisp for about three days, depending upon the variety.

## PUTTING UP

Greens can be frozen beautifully in a soup or puree base; simply cook the recipe to the point where it is part of a stock or puree, then freeze it in an airtight container. When you are ready to make your dish, defrost and continue with the soup or stew. The frozen stock or puree will last for about a year. Herbal greens, such as sorrel, can be dried. It is impossible to can greens.

## SAUTÉED BROCCOLI RABE
### Serves 4

*Most other cooking greens can be prepared precisely the same way. Better yet, combine various greens for interesting flavor.*

> 2 pounds broccoli rabe
> (2 or 3 bunches)
> 2 tablespoons good-quality olive oil
> 2 to 3 garlic cloves, sliced
> Salt and freshly ground black
> pepper

Cut the broccoli rabe flowers and leaves away from the stems. Discard the stems. Rinse and drain the leaves and flowers in a colander.

Heat the olive oil over medium heat in a wide skillet or sauté pan with a tight-fitting lid. Stir in the garlic and cook, stirring, for about 3 minutes, or until lightly golden. Increase heat to high and immediately add the broccoli rabe. Stir the mixture over high heat for about 5 minutes, or until the broccoli rabe softens to the consistency you prefer. Season to taste with salt and pepper and serve hot.

## PREPARING

Wash greens thoroughly in cool water. As with spinach, greens may need to be soaked several times to make sure all traces of sand have been removed. Remove wilted leaves and cut off any root base or thick stem, which is usually bitter and tough. Dry greens thoroughly with paper towels, a dish towel, or a salad spinner.

The proper way to trim and cut up greens is much debated among cooks. Some insist you should always tear leaves by hand; others claim there's nothing wrong with chopping them with a knife or clipping with kitchen shears. It may also depend on the dish. For example, you might tear up

*Baby turnips with their greens*

## CREAM OF SORREL SOUP
### Serves 4

*This rich and sophisticated soup is incredibly delicious served hot or cold.*

½ pound (about 2 large handfuls) fresh sorrel leaves
4 tablespoons (½ stick) butter
4 shallots (or 1 small onion), minced
2 cups chicken broth or water
½ teaspoons salt
Freshly ground black pepper
1 cup heavy cream

Wash the sorrel thoroughly. Shred it finely, discarding the bitter center stems.

Heat butter in a medium nonreactive saucepan over medium heat. Add shallots and sauté for 3 minutes or until the shallots become translucent. Add the sorrel and sauté, stirring constantly, for 3 minutes, or until the sorrel is wilted. (You can freeze the soup at this point; to use, defrost and proceed with the remaining steps.)

Add the chicken broth, salt and pepper to taste, and bring to a boil; simmer for 15 minutes. Add the cream and heat for 1 or 2 minutes (do *not* boil). Serve hot, garnished with minced fresh sorrel. (To serve cold, chill after adding the cream.)

leaves by hand if you are using them in a salad, but use a chef's knife for chopping leaves that will be cooked in a soup.

When preparing strong greens such as beet, dandelion, or turnip greens for a cooked dish, blanch them for a few minutes, depending upon the age and density of the green. This not only takes the harsh flavor out of the green, it prepares it to accept other flavors, such as garlic or herbs, that are part of the final dish.

## SERVING SUGGESTIONS

Tender greens can be mated, raw, in infinite combinations in salads. They can also be blanched, sautéed, or braised to create a side dish or used as an ingredient in other cooked dishes such as omelettes, quiches, stews, and soups. Almost all greens go perfectly with their "significant other." So sprinkle chopped beet greens over cooked beets or stir turnip greens into a cream of turnip soup or mashed turnips.

# Ken Migliorelli

Migliorelli Farm • Dutchess County • Tivoli, New York 12583
Stands at Union Square, World Trade Center, Harlem, and 175th Street (Manhattan)

As Ken Migliorelli says, "They never tear down a house to put in a farm." In fact, Ken has recently built a new house for himself and his family precisely because he knows he is staying on his beautiful farm. The Migliorelli farm, located just east of Tivoli, New York, is one of the participants in Scenic Hudson, a nonprofit, New York State preservation organization that has bought regional farms in order to ensure that the land will never be sold for development. It also ensures that families like the Migliorellis can keep farming, which has been the focus of their lives for three generations.

Ken's grandfather, Angelo Migliorelli, immigrated to the United States from Italy in the 1920s. Amazingly, by 1933, at the height of the Depression, he had managed to save enough money to buy a small truck farm in the Bronx. He specialized in growing cooking greens like broccoli rabe, Swiss chard, kale, and spinach, and then peddled them from a cart around the neighborhood.

Rocco, Angelo's son (and Ken's father) took over the farm in 1954, but by the mid-1960s he could see that their land was being eaten up by superhighways and high-rises. Rocco moved his family to Dutchess County in 1970, when Ken was ten. For the first five years, Rocco managed a dairy farm, but he missed cultivating vegetables, so in 1975, he bought the 125-acre farm in Tivoli. When Ken joined the family business after graduating from Alfred University in 1981, it was struggling, competing with much larger growers in the wholesale markets. Before long, Ken got involved with Greenmarket, and the farm's profits increased.

Today, the Migliorellis still grow beautiful cooking greens. The marvelous irony is that Ken sells them on the streets of New York, just like his grandfather, Angelo, did 70 years ago.

# HERBS

At the height of summer, when fresh herbs arrive in lavish bundles, city folk can be overwhelmed. But, take heart. Herbs are totally sociable plants, and can be used in myriad ways.

## A CULINARY HERBAL

The following herbs are readily available at Greenmarket:

**BASIL.** One of the most esteemed culinary herbs, it is used in many cuisines, particularly Italian. It combines exquisitely with vegetables and other herbs, yet stands majestically on its own, as in a classic pesto. Basil comes in scores of varieties: purple, mammoth, sweet Thai, and lemon are a few available at Greenmarket. In addition to its traditional licorice-like flavor, it can have a lemon, cinnamon, or grassy flavor, depending upon the variety.

**CATNIP.** A member of the mint family, it is primarily used as a treat for spoiled house cats. It is available fresh or dried.

**CHERVIL.** A pretty herb with a sweet, licorice-like flavor. It resembles parsley, and can be substituted for it in most dishes.

**CHIVES.** A member of the onion family, chives have pretty pink or purple flowers that are lovely in bouquets. The stems and leaves, with their peppery onion flavor, can be used in or to garnish soups, sauces, casseroles, omelettes, and other dishes.

**CILANTRO.** The leaves of the coriander plant, which is a member of the carrot family, have a perfumy fragrance and flavor. Cilantro is an important ingredient in many ethnic cuisines, especially Chinese, Indian, Mexican, and Caribbean. It can be used to flavor stir-fries, curries, sauces, soups, salads, and casseroles. The leaves have a perfumy fragrance and flavor.

PESTO

1½ cups Basil
(2 bunches) packed
2 cloves garlic
½ cup olive oil
¼ cup pignoli or walnuts
⅓ cup parmesian or locatelli cheese
Process in food processor until puree texture
Put over pasta
(Excess pesto can be frozen)

*Catnip*

*Chervil*

*Chive flowers*

*Cilantro*

*Dill*

*Fennel*

**DILL.** Dill leaves are dainty, gray-green, and thread-like, and dill flowers resemble yellow Queen Anne's lace. Flowers, stems, leaves, and seeds can all be used to flavor soups, sauces, vegetables, and fish dishes.

**FENNEL.** Fennel seeds and leaves add an anise-like taste to sauces, fish dishes, casseroles, and breads. (For uses of the bulb, see Florence fennel, page 110).

**LEMON BALM.** A dainty herb with

pretty, mint-shaped leaves, it combines well with other herbs, particularly mint, and adds a sophisticated flavor to fruit salads or compotes, teas and tisanes, and a light, lemony flavor to fish and chicken. The leaves make an attractive garnish.

**LEMONGRASS.** A long, blade-shaped green that has a distinctive lemony fra-

grance and flavor. It is a common flavoring in Thai food, can be used to season fish or chicken, and makes an interesting addition to salads and teas.

**LEMON VERBENA.** An elegant herb with small, pointy leaves and a lemony fragrance and flavor. It can be used in any dish that welcomes a fresh lemon scent or flavor, including cocktails, teas, puddings, cakes, ice creams, and fruit compotes.

**LOVAGE.** Lovage has dark green leaves and a strong celery-like flavor that stands up well in soups, stews, salads, and cooked vegetables. Dried lovage seeds are sold commercially as celery seed.

**MARJORAM.** A relative of oregano, marjoram is an integral part of Italian, Provençal, Moroccan, and Spanish cuisines. The leaves have a sweet/spicy flavor. Use them to flavor vegetables, sauces, stuffings, fish, poultry, and meats. The flowers make a delightful garnish.

**MINT.** At Greenmarket, many of mint's 600 varieties are available, including spearmint and peppermint. Mint is used to flavor grilled meats (lamb), vegetables (peas), sweets, cocktails (mint juleps), and teas. It is frequently used to "cool" spicy dishes and to garnish fruit compotes and cakes.

*Lemon verbena*   *Lovage*

*Marjoram*

*Mint*

**OREGANO.** Oregano is one of the distinctive flavors of Italian cuisine. It can be used to season sauces, grilled meats, vegetables, and breads, including pizza and focaccia. Oregano also blends well with other savory herbs, especially marjoram and thyme.

*Italian Parsley*

*Rosemary*

**PARSLEY.** Parsley is available in two varieties: curly parsley, which has dark green, tightly curled leaves, and Italian parsley, which has flatter, paler green leaves. Both are mild-flavored, although curly parsley is slightly more "grassy" in taste.

**ROSEMARY.** Rosemary has distinctive thread-like leaves and a pungent fragrance. It gives a special flavor to grilled meats, as well as to potatoes and other vegetables. It also makes a beautiful garnish.

**SAGE.** Oblong, gray-green sage leaves are hardy and hold their shape in salads and infused vinegars and give strong flavor to meats, stuffings, rice dishes, and breads.

**SAVORY.** Closely related to mint, savory comes in summer or winter varieties. (Winter is stronger than summer.) Savory has a pungent, minty, thyme-like flavor, and is

*Sage*

*Savory*

best used to flavor grilled meats, pâtés, and cooked vegetables.

**TARRAGON.** Tarragon is a classic French herb, and the identifying flavor in béarnaise sauce and a traditional French fines herbes. It adds subtle sweetness, particularly to egg dishes, cheese dishes, poultry, grilled lamb and pork. It also adds a beautiful flavor to a fruit compote.

**THYME.** Thyme is a basic element of French bouquet garni (the others being parsley and bay leaves) and serves as a standard ingredient in stocks, marinades, stuffings, sauces, and soups. It has a pungent flavor and mingles nicely with poultry, game, fish, and cooked vegetables.

*Tarragon*        *Thyme*

---

## LEMONGRASS TEA
### Makes 6 cups

*This tea is at once soothing and stimulating—a nice tea to have in the late afternoon for a pick-me-up. It is also delicious iced.*

3  tablespoons crushed lemongrass
3  teaspoons crushed lemon thyme
6  cups boiling water
    Sugar or honey and cream, or
    whole lemon balm leaves (if iced)

Place the crushed leaves in a tea caddie or loose in a teapot. Pour the boiling water over the leaves. Allow the tea to steep for about 5 minutes. Serve very hot with sweetener and cream, or iced, garnished with whole lemon balm leaves.

---

## SELECTING

Choose herbs that look fresh and are brightly colored. Consider them as you would fresh flowers, and select those that have not begun to wilt or turn brown.

## STORING

Wrap fresh herbs in a damp paper towel and store inside a plastic bag in the refrigerator, or arrange them as a bouquet in a vase of cool water and store the vase in the refrigerator. Use them, including freezing or drying them, within two days or they will lose their flavor.

## PUTTING UP

Herbs can be frozen, dried, or preserved in vinegar or oil.

**FREEZING** is the easiest method for preserving herbs. Simply mince them, place them in an airtight bag or container, and freeze. For premeasured herbs for use in soups and stews, place 1 tablespoon of minced herbs into sections of an ice cube tray, fill with water, then freeze. Or freeze fresh herbs in butter: Cream 1 stick (¼ pound) butter with 1 tablespoon of chopped herbs of your choice. Form into a log, wrap it in plastic, label, and freeze.

**DRYING** herbs is almost as easy as freezing, although it takes more time. Depending upon the size and thickness of the leaves, herbs will dry at different rates, so separate them accordingly.

To dry stemmed herbs, tie them with string into small bunches and hang the bunches upside down in a dry, airy place for about three weeks.

To dry herbs in a conventional oven, place leaves on a piece of cheesecloth or brown paper over a rack. Preheat the oven to 175°F, place the rack in the oven, turn the oven off, and allow the herbs to dry until they are easily broken with your fingers.

To dry herbs in a microwave oven, place leaves between two paper towels and set the microwave on High for one minute. If the herb is not bone-dry, continue drying at 30-second intervals until the leaves are easily broken with your fingers.

When the herbs are thoroughly dry, place the dried leaves, as uncrumbled as possible, in airtight containers. (Crush the leaves just before using them for best flavor.) Store them in a dry place, away from heat or moisture, or freeze them. Dried herbs will hold their flavor for a year.

PRESERVING herbs in vinegars, vegetable oils, butters, and, in some cases—such as with mint and rosemary—as jellies offers excellent options for using herbs as flavorings.

## PREPARING

Just before cooking with fresh herbs, wash them gently in cool water and blot them dry with paper towels. When chopping them, use a very sharp chef's knife or kitchen shears to avoid bruising the leaves.

Add herbs to cooked dishes at the last minute so the flavor is not cooked away. When adding herbs to cold dishes, such as potato salads or salad dressings, allow the dish to rest for about two hours so that the flavor has time to penetrate.

*Black peppermint*

In most cases, dried herbs have a stronger flavor than fresh. When substituting dried for fresh herbs, use about half the amount.

## SERVING SUGGESTIONS

Using herbs is the simplest and yet the most sophisticated way to enhance any dish. Virtually any dish can be creatively flavored or garnished with fresh herbs.

When fresh herbs are abundant, dry them and make holiday presents of herb blends or herb-flavored vinegars and oils. Decorative jars and bottles are available at housewares and gourmet shops.

W S S F

# THE D'ATTOLICO FAMILY

D'ATTOLICO'S ORGANIC FARM • Orange County • Pine Island, New York 10969
Stands at Union Square (Manahattan); Borough Hall and Grand Army Plaza (Brooklyn)

Unlike many of the growers who come from old family farms, Vince D'Attolico grew up in Brooklyn. He was trained as an electrical contractor and worked hard at it for years; however, his sanctuary was to work in his garden. When the economy took dip in the mid-1970s, Vince bought a small, 12-acre farm in the "Black Dirt" region of Orange County and moved his family up there permanently.

Vince established some firm rules for himself and his farm. First, he kept his farm small, cultivating only about 10 acres and rotating crops to keep the soil viable. He insisted on farming completely organically, growing beautiful greens, fresh herbs, a remarkable array of

sprouts, as well as celery, carrots, beets, garlic, and other vegetables. Vince also felt strongly that his business remain "strictly family."

*Vince D'Attolico with his grandson, Jesse*

Vince began selling at Greenmarket in 1982, and for many years was a popular figure at the market and developed a devoted clientele. Although he allowed that he would never be rich, Vince loved farming, was confident he could make a decent living, and best of all, had something better than riches: peace of mind.

Vince died suddenly in 1997. His many friends, and certainly his family, were shocked and saddened, but they kept on. Vince's wife, Joan, and son, Vinnie, Jr., still manage the stand at Union Square, and his daughter, Sue, runs the stand at Grand Army Plaza. D'Attolico greens, sprouts, and vegetables are as fresh and beautiful as ever. Vince would be proud.

*Joan D'Attolico*      *Sue D'Attolico*

# HONEY & OTHER BEE PRODUCTS

Honey and bee pollen are products created by perhaps the most creative, industrious, and fascinating farmer on the face of the earth: the simple bee. The apiarists (those human farmers who cultivate bees and harvest their products) are quite fascinating as well!

## VARIETIES

The following products of bees are available at Greenmarket:

**BEE POLLEN.** Bee pollen is the powdery or grainy substance that is produced by plants and collected by bees. Often referred to as nature's "perfect" food because it has 22 nutrients and six times more protein than beef, it is used to increase energy and strength. It can be taken by the spoonful or in tea. It helps combat fatigue, depression, and some diseases.

**BEE PROPOLIS.** This resinous substance, collected from plants by bees, is used with beeswax in the construction of beehives. It is a powerful natural antibiotic. It is usually sold as a salve or balm, and can be used on abrasions and bruises.

**BEESWAX.** This yellow wax secreted by bees to build their hives is sold in blocks or as beeswax candles at Greenmarket.

**HONEY.** This is the yellow, golden, or brownish liquid produced by bees from the nectar of flowers. Honey is a natural sugar.

**ROYAL JELLY.** Royal jelly is a milky substance made by worker bees and fed to the queen. It is very rich in vitamins and minerals. The royal jelly needs to be combined with honey to preserve its potency, and apiarists sell it as a honey-butter that can be eaten by the spoonful or spread on a muffin or toast.

## SELECTING

All bee products should come in tightly sealed containers. Ask the apiarist for information and guidance.

## STORING

Store honey at room temperature, as refrigeration promotes crystallization. If honey crystallizes, remove the lid and place the jar in warm water, or put one cup of the honey in a microwave-safe container, and heat at High for 30 seconds. Store bee pollen and bee propolis at room temperature as you would vitamins. Store royal jelly in the refrigerator.

## PREPARING AND USING

Honey can be substituted for about half the amount of sugar in many recipes. In baking, you may need to reduce the amount of liquid if honey is used. Honey can be used as a flavoring in sauces (barbecue sauce, ketchup, mustard sauce), salad dressings, and butters. Take the other products as you would vitamins.

---

## ROASTED PEARS WITH HONEY & PECORINO TOSCANO
### Serves 4

*This recipe comes from Mario Batali, the chef of Po and Babbo in Greenwich Village and an avid supporter of Greenmarket.*

- 4 large pears, Bosc or Anjou, not quite ripe
- 1 cup Chianti or other dry red wine
- 1 cup sugar
- 1 cup honey (ideally chestnut or orange-blossom honey)
- 8 ounces Pecorino Toscano in a single chunk

Preheat the oven to 400°F. Trim the bottoms of the pears so they will stand up. Arrange them upright in a small baking dish. Pour the wine and sugar into the dish around the pears. Place in the oven and bake until soft, about 40 minutes.

To serve, place each pear in the center of a dessert plate. Drizzle the honey over the pears and spoon the wine sauce around the base of each. Using a peeler, shave pieces of Pecorino over the pears and serve.

---

# HORSERADISH & OTHER ROOTS

Most of us grew up with a nodding relationship with jarred horseradish. Still, we may be mystified when presented with fresh horseradish, not to mention other roots like burdock, salsify, or parsley root. These are fascinating, flavorful vegetables and well worth exploring.

## VARIETIES

**HORSERADISH.** Technically an herb (and an ancient one), horseradish is cultivated primarily for its long, beige root that is extremely hot and flavorful. (The leaves can also be used for flavoring.) It is usually made into a relish and used as a condiment for roasts and vegetable dishes.

**BURDOCK.** Cultivated in Japan as Gobo, in our region, it has long been considered a wild root, and growers have only recently begun cultivating it. Burdock has a sweet, earthy flavor and crisp texture. It is delicious shredded or chopped in soups and salads. Use it as you would parsnips or salsify.

**SALSIFY.** Called "oyster plant" because theoretically it tastes like raw oysters, salsify is a white-fleshed root with gray or pale brown skin. It can be steamed or boiled as a side dish or used to flavor soups and stews.

**PARSLEY ROOT.** Shaped like a parsnip, it tastes like a cross between carrot and celery. Although it is related to parsley, it is cultivated for its root; its feathery leaves cannot be substituted for ordinary parsley.

## Selecting

Choose roots that are firm and seem crisp, with smooth, unwrinkled, and unblemished skin. Horseradish loses its "fire" and flavor quickly, so buy only small amounts at a time.

## Storing

Store all roots, unwashed, in a plastic bag in the refrigerator. They will stay crisp, fresh, and flavorful for about seven days.

## Putting Up

A little horseradish goes a long way, but if you are a horseradish fanatic you might want to preserve fresh horseradish to use as a relish or for flavoring when pickling other vegetables. (To preserve it, simply add one part grated horseradish to two parts white wine vinegar and allow it to marinate in the refrigerator for two weeks.) Burdock, salsify, and parsley root can be canned or frozen as purees. All roots can be dried.

## Preparing

Like hot peppers and onions, horseradish can burn the skin and cause eyes to water. To avoid the agony, grate horseradish with

a fine blade of a food processor. If you do grate by hand, set the grater in a bowl to catch juices and try to work at arms length to avoid the fumes. In either case, scrub the root thoroughly before grating.

To prepare burdock, salsify, or parsley root, scrub the root thoroughly and scrape as you would a carrot or a parsnip. All these roots are strongly flavored and should be coarsely chopped or julienned before being added to a dish. The roots can be boiled, steamed, braised, or roasted.

## Serving Suggestions

Combine a teaspoon or two of preserved horseradish with whipped cream, sour cream, yogurt, or crème fraîche for a delicious, spicy accompaniment to roasts, game, potatoes, and other root vegetables.

Add grated or chopped salsify, burdock, or parsley root to soups, stews, casseroles, and roasted vegetable mélanges. They can also be pureed or baked in a sauce and served as a side dish.

# HOUSEPLANTS

Houseplants are basically plants that can be grown in an ordinary indoor environment as opposed to a greenhouse, and do not require a tremendous amount of expert care.

## VARIETIES

The many types of houseplants available at Greenmarket include:

**AFRICAN VIOLET.** A pretty and popular plant with velvety green leaves and flowers that range in color from purple, blue, and lavender to pink, coral, and white. It flowers year-round.

**BEGONIA.** A plant with bright flowers in shades of red, pink, orange, and yellow. It provides lovely color in winter.

**CACTI & SUCCULENTS.** Plants that come in many varieties, including yucca and flowering cacti, and require little care.

*Begonia*          *Cacti*

**COLEUS.** An easy-to-grow plant with variegated foliage that can be maroon, crimson, or yellow.

**FERNS.** Many varieties, including Boston fern, holly fern, staghorn fern, rabbit's foot fern. Ferns need lots of sun and moisture.

**GLOXINIA.** A relative of the African violet, with colorful bell-shaped flowers and dark green, fuzzy leaves.

**PHILODENDRON.** Probably the most common houseplant. Easy to maintain, it has bright green, heart-shaped leaves.

## SELECTING

Choose young yet established plants. They should look fresh and "bushy" (depending upon type), with compact foliage. Avoid plants that appear wilted or that have brown spots which could indicate possible insect infestation or disease. Think about your personal needs and the conditions in your house, including light and air. Remember, some plants may be toxic to children or pets.

## CARE

The amount of water, sunlight, and temperature needed depends upon the plant. Ask the farmer or consult a good plant guide for details.

Make sure the plant is in a pot that suits its size, variety, and drainage requirements. In most cases, keep the atmosphere moist. Pinch off leaves to make plants bushier, more graceful, and compact.

Wash plant leaves regularly to remove oily silt. Use a teaspoon of milk, liquid soap, or commercial plant soap in the water.

Turn and/or move plants regularly to make sure they get enough light. Remove dead leaves and stems.

Talk to your plants.

## DISPLAYING

Combine plants with foliage of different shades, shapes, textures, and colors; conversely, combine several of the same variety, such as cacti or types of ferns. Mass plants to create a "plant center" in a room or space. Use houseplants in hanging baskets and window boxes together with flowers. Use houseplants in kitchens and bathrooms, as well as throughout the rest of the apartment or house.

# Jams, Jellies, & Preserves

Several Greenmarket farmers sell jams, mustards, oils, vinegars, and other preserves. According to the market rules, such items must be prepared by the seller and contain only fresh produce from his or her own farm or from a regional farmer.

## Varieties

**Chutney.** Chutney is a concoction of fruits, vegetables, vinegar, sugar, and spices. It is a classic accompaniment to Indian curries, and goes well with cheeses.

**Fruit butter.** This is made from fruit, especially apples, pears, peaches, apricots, and quince, that is very slowly simmered down to its essence.

**Jam.** Jam is fruit that has been cooked down, usually with pectin and sugar added, until it is very soft.

**Jelly.** Jelly is a clear mixture made from the juice of the fruit together with pectin and sugar. Jelly is firmer than jam.

**Marmalade.** Marmalade is a cross between jam and jelly and is made from the rind of soft fruits, especially citrus fruits and quince.

**Mustard.** A condiment made with mustard seed, vinegar, herbs, and flavorings.

**Oil.** Olive oil can be flavored with garlic, herbs, and certain vegetables. Several farmers offer many styles of flavored oils.

**Vinegar.** Vinegar can be made from fruit juices, and can be flavored with vegetables, fruits, herbs, and spices.

## Storing

Most preserves have been processed in vacuum-packed jars, and can be stored at room temperature for at least a year, if not indefinitely. After the jar is opened, it should be refrigerated, and will keep for several weeks. Products that have not been processed should be refrigerated and will keep for about a month.

# BETH LINSKEY

BETH'S FARM KITCHEN • Columbia County
Stuyvesant Falls, New York 12174
Stands at Union Square and World Trade Center (Manhattan)

"My mother sent me to college, and I find myself working as a street vendor." Not that Beth Linskey minds. In fact, she loves her work.

A native of Chicago, Beth majored in home economics at Rosary College in River Forest, Illinois, then moved to New York City. In 1980, she and her husband bought a house in the Hudson Valley. Since he was working in New York and she had started a catering business (which included making jams and jellies), they maintained an apartment in the city.

Beth started selling at Greenmarket in 1983, and her preserves business really took off. (Until then, preserves had been only a sideline to catering.) Although she didn't grow fruit herself, she could buy all she needed from her upstate neighbors. From the Samascott farm down the road she got apples and strawberries, and from Chip Kent she got quince and berries.

Like all newcomers at Greenmarket, she had to "pay her dues," selling at some of the smaller markets. It took a couple of years before she graduated to the Union Square market. Beth's original "test kitchen" was small as well. She started out cooking on an apartment-sized electric stove in a typical New York Pullman kitchen. Today, she still cooks in her own home, although the kitchen is much bigger and she has two large stoves and 14 burners. Still, she cooks only in small batches, creating about a dozen jars of jam in a batch.

After 16 years, Beth has a thriving mail-order business and also sells regularly to various New York City and upstate restaurants in addition to at her stand at Greenmarket. However, Beth says she would not be in business without Greenmarket. She loves the contact with people and cherishes her special customers who come back every week. Even at the World Trade Center, a seemingly impersonal place, the customers are warm and human. In fact, they are friends.

# JERUSALEM ARTICHOKES

Also known as sunchokes, these homely little vegetables are actually the tubers of a variety of sunflower. They look like a cross between a small potato and a gingerroot, and have a sweet, nutty flavor and crisp texture. They are harvested from late summer through autumn, and, like other tubers, are available at Greenmarket throughout the winter.

## SELECTING

Although they are naturally bumpy, look for tubers that are relatively smooth and free of wrinkles, blemishes, or bruises. They should be firm, not spongy, and pale brown in color, with no greenish tinge or sign of sprouts or mold.

## STORING

Store sunchokes in a plastic bag in the crisper of the refrgerator. (They can also be stored in cold storage.) Sunchokes will keep for about two weeks.

## PUTTING UP

Sunchokes don't can, freeze, or dry well. To preserve them as a pickle-like condiment, combine thinly sliced raw sunchokes in a jar with brine from commercial pickles.

## PREPARING

Much of the nutritional value of Jerusalem artichokes (they are rich in iron) is in the skin, so ideally they should be prepared with the skins on. Scrub them carefully; if you do peel them, use a vegetable peeler and place the peeled sunchokes in cool water acidulated with white vinegar or lemon juice to prevent discoloration. Cook them in a nonreactive pan; aluminum or iron pans will alter their color. Sunchokes can be baked, boiled, steamed, braised, sautéed, or stir-fried.

## SERVING SUGGESTIONS

Sunchokes can be eaten raw or cooked. Most people prefer them combined with other vegetables (potatoes, turnips, parsnips, rutabaga, and other wild roots); potato-and-sunchoke puree is delicious. Still, cooked sunchokes can be served alone and their crisp and nutty flavor goes especially nicely with carrots, Brussels sprouts, and broccoli. To serve them raw, blanch them for 2 minutes, then peel them. Thinly sliced, raw sunchokes are tasty in slaws or salads.

---

### JERUSALEM ARTICHOKE MÉLANGE
**Serves 6**

2  Jerusalem artichokes
2  medium parsnips
2  medium red potatoes
6  tablespoons butter
3  tablespoons fresh lemon juice
   Salt and freshly ground pepper
¼  cup freshly chopped parsley

---

Peel the sunchokes and parsnips and chop coarsely. Scrub the potatoes, but do not peel; chop them coarsely. Combine the vegetables in a large, heavy saucepan and cover with water. Bring to a boil and simmer until the vegetables are tender, about 20 minutes. Drain.

In a heavy saucepan, melt the butter. Add the lemon juice, salt and pepper to taste, and parsley. Add the cooked vegetables and toss. Serve immediately.

*A sunflower bud, a relative of the Jerusalem artichoke*

# KOHLRABI

Kohlrabi is the ugly stepsister of the family. It's a weird-looking vegetable with a purplish-green bulb, and leaves that sprout from the globe. Its name, from the German, means "cabbage-turnip" and, in fact, kohlrabi looks like a cross between a cabbage and a turnip, although its mild flavor is more radish-like. Like many homely relations, once you get past kohlrabi's appearance and eccentricities, it is a special vegetable.

## SELECTING

Kohlrabi is at its tastiest when it is young and small, in this region usually in June or July. (Kohlrabi is available at Greenmarket from June through late September, although by late summer the globes are more mature and, therefore, are less tender and have a stronger flavor.) For most simple dishes, choose globes that are no larger than 3 inches in diameter and make sure the leaves look fresh. Plan for about three small globes per person. If you plan to cook kohlrabi with cheese, cream, or some other sauce, the larger globes can be delicious.

## STORING

Remove the leaves before storing. Store the kohlrabi bulbs in a perforated plastic bag in the crisper of the refrigerator. They will keep for about five days.

## PUTTING UP

Kohlrabi is a watery vegetable, with a texture not unlike a radish. As a result, it does not freeze or dry well; it is too strong-flavored to can.

## PREPARING

Preparing kohlrabi may seem a bit daunting at first glance. However, you'll quickly see that preparing a kohlrabi globe is fairly easy. Using a sharp, non-carbon steel knife, trim the stems and leaves from the globes. The edible part of the kohlrabi is the pure white globe, but the globe is encased by an outer "leafy" skin (with the texture of a cabbage leaf) that must be removed before or after the kohlrabi is cooked. This can require some effort. To peel the skin, use a paring knife or vegetable peeler. Be sure to remove all vestiges of the purple leaves, which can be bitter.

## SERVING SUGGESTIONS

Young kohlrabi globes can be served lightly blanched and sliced as part of a crudité platter. Chilled, roasted, or braised, kohlrabi serves as an interesting accompaniment to roasted meats, especially ham, venison, and game. Thinly sliced or chopped, kohlrabi adds an interesting turnip-like flavor to soups and stews. Like cauliflower, kohlrabi combines well with cream and various cheeses and can be served in a casserole or as a side dish.

---

### BRAISED BABY KOHLRABI WITH TURNIPS & CARROTS
**Serves 4 to 6**

| | |
|---|---|
| 4 to 6 | baby kohlrabi |
| 10 or 12 | baby turnips |
| 4 to 6 | baby carrots |
| 2 | tablespoons chopped fresh tarragon |
| | Butter |
| | Salt and freshly ground pepper |

Clean and trim the kohlrabi; unless it is very young, slice or julienne the globes. Clean and trim the turnips and carrots. Place the vegetables in a shallow saucepan, add an inch or 2 of water, and simmer for about 20 minutes, or until tender. Drain. Add fresh tarragon, butter, and salt and pepper to taste and toss to combine. Serve hot.

---

# LEEKS

Leeks look somewhat like mature scallions, but, in fact, are only cousins to the onion family. (Scallions, on the other hand, are immature onions.) Still, leeks

have an oniony flavor, although they tend to be milder and sweeter. Like onions, they are often used to add flavor to soups, stews, and casseroles, but they can be delicious served on their own or combined with other winter vegetables. (Vichyssoise, a soup of potatoes and leeks, is perhaps the most famous dish using leeks.)

## SELECTING

Leeks have green leaves, a long white root with a slight bulb on the end, and a "beard" of rootlets. They are generally sold in bunches of four or five. Look for bright green, crisp leaves without signs of wilting or brown spots. The bulbs should be straight, clean, and crisp-looking, about 1 to 1½ inches in diameter, and white. If leeks grow too large, they become woody and tasteless and can sometimes split. The fringe of rootlets should look fresh.

## STORING

Store the leeks, unwashed and untrimmed, in a plastic bag in the refrigerator. Unlike mature onions, leeks cannot be stored dry (in cold storage) and should not be stored with other fruits and vegetables, because their odor will spread to the other foods. Leeks can keep for five to seven days.

## PUTTING UP

It is possible to can or freeze leeks, but because they contain a significant amount of water, they loose their crisp texture and much of their flavor.

## PREPARING

Leeks require careful cleaning because they can harbor sand and dirt in their tight layers. Remove withered outer leaves, then trim off the green tops and the rootlets. Split the bulb lengthwise, pull the leaves apart, and rinse them thoroughly.

Leeks can be braised (in stock, white wine, or butter), roasted (usually with other root vegetables, such as carrots or parsnips), steamed, or boiled. They should be cooked until just tender to preserve a delectable crunch. (If they are overcooked, they become mushy.)

## SERVING SUGGESTIONS

Leeks can be served braised, as a side dish, either plain or with a sauce such as a light lemon-butter sauce, a vinaigrette, or a cream sauce. Leeks combine well with other vegetables, particularly winter root vegetables, and are also delicious with mushrooms and tomatoes. Leeks can be added to soups, stews, stir-fries, and casseroles instead of (or in addition to) onions or scallions.

## BRAISED LEEKS WITH LEMON THYME
### Serves 4

*Lemon thyme adds a pleasant lemon-licorice flavor to the warm leeks. It's quite lovely.*

- 2 tablespoons good-quality olive oil
- 2 tablespoons butter
- 4 to 6 leeks, trimmed, cleaned, and quartered lengthwise
- ½ cup chicken broth
  Salt and freshly ground black pepper
- 1 tablespoon chopped fresh lemon thyme
  Juice of 1 lemon (about 1 tablespoon)

In a heavy saucepan or deep skillet, heat the olive oil and butter over medium heat. Add the leeks and sauté for about 5 minutes. Add the chicken broth, and salt and pepper to taste, and simmer until the leeks are tender, about 15 minutes more.

Transfer the leeks to a serving platter. Sprinkle with the lemon thyme and lemon juice. Serve warm.

# LETTUCES

Many varieties of lettuce are grown in our region, and many of those are available at Greenmarket, from the familiar Bibb to the more unusual mâche. Sometimes it is difficult to define the difference between a "lettuce" and a "green" (or a "lettuce," a "green," and an "herb," for that matter). For this book, greens of the species *Lactuca* or *Lactuca satina* (true lettuces) are listed under "Lettuces" and all other greens can be found under "Greens," page 124–133.

Lettuces (and many other greens) are ready as early as mid-May, are piled high by mid-June, and remain available—due to multiple plantings and greenhouse growing by some farmers—until late autumn.

## VARIETIES

Many varieties of lettuce are available at Greenmarket. Your choice depends upon taste and the dish you are preparing.

**BIBB LETTUCE.** Bibb lettuce has rather a small head, and the leaves, though delicate, are not as soft as Boston lettuce leaves. Bibb lettuce is perhaps the most common lettuce for all-American tossed salads.

**BOSTON (OR BUTTER) LETTUCE.** Boston lettuce is characterized by its loose head and green, soft leaves. This is a tender, sweet lettuce that should be dressed with a delicate vinaigrette and combined with lighter main dishes, such as freshly grilled fish. This is a marvelous lettuce for tossed

salads, but usually needs to be combined with other, firmer lettuces for the salad to remain fresh and lively looking.

**FRISÉE.** Sometimes called curly endive,

frisée has tight, curly leaves, a pale, creamy green color, and a rather strong, bitter flavor. In salads, it carries (and can be combined with) stronger flavors and textures such ingredients as lardons or cheeses.

**ICEBERG (OR CRISPHEAD) LETTUCE.** Iceberg is the lettuce many of us were forced to eat as children, and hated. It comes in large, pale green, tight heads, has watery leaves, and is hearty, as lettuces go. Although often associated with watery, tasteless salad, iceberg lettuce has its place in a sophisticated kitchen. Since it holds up well, it is ideal for adding crunch to sandwiches. It is also a classic garnish for Mexican tacos, and makes a nice lettuce cup for salsa, fruit, crudités, or composed vegetable platters. It is the best lettuce to use as a wrapper for stuffed dishes.

**GARDEN (OR LEAF) LETTUCE.** Leaf lettuce is perhaps the most popular lettuce in

our region. It has large, curly leaves, and is at its best when it is ultrafresh, which is only a day or two. It makes a pretty and tasty green salad on its own, or combines well with other lettuces, greens, herbs, and vegetables because of its vivid color and because it adds flavor and body to the salad.

**MÂCHE.** Mâche, also known as lamb's lettuce or corn salad, is a very mild lettuce that combines beautifully in salads, especially with Boston lettuce.

**OAK LEAF LETTUCE.** Oak leaf lettuce gets its name from the shape of its leaves, which resemble the leaves of an oak tree. It comes in small, loose heads, and has a relatively strong flavor. It's a pretty addition to a tossed green salad.

**RED LEAF LETTUCE.** Red leaf lettuce is a variety of garden lettuce that boasts leaves tinged with a rusty red color. The flavor is the same as garden lettuce, and red leaf combines with it to make an extremely attractive salad or garnish.

**ROMAINE.** Romaine lettuce comes in oblong, often very full heads, and has hearty, flavorful leaves. It is the lettuce used in a classic Caesar salad because it can carry the weight and stronger flavors in the dressing.

It combines well with other lettuces and greens, particularly the softer-leaved, milder ones, to give firmness and fuller flavor to salads.

## SELECTING

Look for bright colors, no sign of wilting or decay, and a fresh fragrance.

## STORING

Before storing, remove any bands or string that might bruise the greens, and discard any tired outer leaves. Most farmers suggest that lettuce be stored unwashed and loose. Layer and wrap the leaves in paper towels or a dish towel, and store in the refrigerator crisper. Lettuce will stay fresh and crisp for about three days, more or less depending upon the variety.

## PUTTING UP

Enjoy lettuce fresh. It cannot be frozen, dried, or preserved.

## PREPARING

To prepare, wash the leaves thoroughly in cool water, remove wilted leaves, and cut off any root base or thick stem. Lettuce is softer than other greens, and

should be handled gently and should not be soaked. Dry the leaves thoroughly using a salad spinner, paper towel, or soft dish towel, because excess water dilutes dressings and sauces.

The best method of trimming and cutting up lettuce and salad greens is much debated among cooks. Some insist you should always tear leaves by hand; others claim there's nothing wrong with chopping them with a knife or clipping stems

## WILTED LETTUCE SALAD
### Serves 4

*This dish is rather like a mild, more subtle version of a classic spinach salad.*

1 head iceberg lettuce
1 cup sliced fresh mushrooms
2 hard-boiled eggs, sliced
8 slices (about ½ pound) bacon
¼ cup olive oil
1 small onion, minced
2 garlic cloves, minced
¼ cup cider vinegar
2 teaspoons Dijon mustard
  Salt and freshly ground pepper

Wash, dry, and cut the lettuce into bite-sized pieces; place in a large salad bowl. Add the sliced mushrooms and toss. Reserving a few egg slices for a garnish, toss the remaining slices into the salad.

In a medium frying pan, fry the bacon until crisp. Transfer bacon to paper towels to drain; crumble and set aside. Add the olive oil to the rendered fat and heat over medium heat until bubbling. Add the onion and garlic and sauté until translucent. Add the vinegar and cook briefly, until the vinegar begins to steam. Stir in the mustard, then immediately pour the hot dressing over the lettuce. Add the bacon, and salt and pepper to taste, and toss. Garnish with egg slices and serve.

with kitchen shears. Usually, the choice depends on the lettuce, the dish being prepared, and personal preference.

## SERVING SUGGESTIONS

Lettuces, together with other greens, herbs, and vegetables (as well as meats, cheeses, and eggs), can be mated in infinite combinations in salads. They can also be blanched, sautéed, or braised for use as a side dish, or used in various other cooked dishes, such as omelettes, quiches, and certain soups.

*Mâche*

### AUTUMN GREEN SALAD WITH PEARS
#### Serves 6

*This simple salad is especially attractive because of the beautiful lettuces and is very tasty with roasted chicken or duck.*

| | |
|---|---|
| 1 | head oak leaf lettuce |
| 1 | head red leaf lettuce |
| 3 | medium pears |
| ½ | cup olive oil |
| 2 | tablespoons balsamic vinegar |
| 2 | garlic cloves, minced |
| 2 | teaspoons grainy mustard |
| | Salt and freshly ground pepper |
| 1 | cup whole shelled walnuts |

Wash and dry the lettuce thoroughly and tear into bite-sized pieces. Peel, core, and slice the pears. In a large salad bowl, combine the olive oil, vinegar, garlic, mustard, and salt and pepper to taste. Add the lettuces, pear slices, and walnuts, and toss to combine. Serve immediately on chilled plates.

○ ◐ ◐ ◐
W S S F

# DAVID YEN

PNS HYGIENIC FARM • Suffolk County • Patchogue, New York 11772
Stand at Union Square (Manhattan)

David Yen is one of the most fascinating growers at Greenmarket. Aside from the fact that he grows a stunning array of both traditional and exotic greens, David is one of just a handful of growers who, because he grows extensively in greenhouses, offers fresh lettuce and other greens virtually throughout the winter.

David emigrated to the United States from China in 1977. He settled on Long Island and in the first years that he lived here, worked in the jewelry business. Gradually, he became more and more interested in agriculture and finally, eight years ago, bought a 20-acre farm in Patchogue, Long Island. Together with his wife Julie, he very successfully farms several fields as well as about four acres within greenhouses.

David specializes in a fascinating array of Asian greens and vegetables, including Chinese mustard greens, wasabi (Japanese horseradish), mibuna and mizuna (very flavorful Asian salad greens), Japanese spinach, Japanese culy (a variety of seedless cucumber), and Shanghai (or baby) bok choy. David cultivates soybeans outdoors in the field, picks them in September, quick-freezes them, then sells them throughout winter. David has a strong interest in the medicinal uses of the herbs and greens he cultivates (for example, girula, a green that helps ease premenstrual syndrome), and he generously (and gregariously) shares his knowledge with customers.

In addition to Asian vegetables, David also cultivates many interesting varieties of Western vegetables, such as grape tomatoes, and greens, such as baby arugula, a delicate frisée lettuce, and four or five types of kale.

David Yen brings extensive knowledge of Eastern plants and planting to Greenmarket, and his contributions are much appreciated by New York consumers.

# Maple Syrup

Upstate New York and Vermont are well-known as the sources for the most exquisite maple syrup, or "sweetwater," as the American Indians called it. Thus, it is not surprising that New York State maple syrup is a staple at Greenmarket. The "sugaring-off season" begins in February, when the days begin to become warmer, and lasts until spring, or as long as the nights stay cold. During those last weeks of winter, maple syrup is featured at Greenmarket, although, in fact, it is available all year long.

## Making Maple Syrup

Not so many years ago, sap from maple trees was tapped using a metal spile and a bucket. Today, however, most maple producers have speeded up the process by connecting their trees (collectively known as a sugar bush) with a network of lightweight plastic tubing. Through these tubes, the sap flows into vats or is pumped into a sugarhouse. When the sap arrives in the sugarhouse, it is mostly water. To create the syrup, the sap must be boiled down or evaporated. (This is done with sophisticated equipment.)

The statistics connected to the creation of maple syrup are quite astonishing. For example, it takes 40 gallons of sap to make one gallon of syrup, and an average maple tree yields about 10 gallons of sap or one quart of syrup. To put it another way, it takes many trees and much work to produce a small amount of sweetwater.

## Selecting

According to New York State laws, all maple syrup sold must meet certain standards, be graded according to three particular categories, and be appropriately labeled when sold commercially.

## New York Grades

**GRADE A LIGHT AMBER.** The lightest of the three classifications; it has a mild and delicate flavor.

**GRADE A MEDIUM AMBER.** A bit darker in color; it has a full and richer maple flavor.

**GRADE A DARK AMBER.** The darkest in color of the three grades; it has the strongest maple flavor.

**NEW YORK STATE EXTRA DARK.** A special class for syrups used for cooking.

## STORING

Store unopened jars or cans of maple syrup in a cool, dry place. After the container has been opened, syrup should be refrigerated, and will keep for a year. If mold forms on the surface of the syrup, simply remove the mold, heat the syrup to boiling, skim the surface of the syrup, and pour into a sterilized container.

## PUTTING UP

Maple syrup can be used as part of the sugar- or syrup-packing when canning fruits. If a syrup container has been opened, some of the syrup can be frozen in an airtight plastic container for as long as a year. Defrost the syrup in the refrigerator.

## PREPARING

Maple sugar is very sweet. When substituting maple syrup for sugar in a recipe, use about 25 percent less syrup than sugar. Also, bear in mind that the flavor of maple syrup is strong and distinctive, so be conservative when considering substituting maple syrup for refined sugar.

## SERVING SUGGESTIONS

Maple syrup is the classic topping for pancakes, waffles, and French toast, but can also be drizzled over ice cream, yogurt, baked fruit, and other desserts. Maple syrup can be substituted for sugar in many recipes, especially old-fashioned American recipes like Boston baked beans, glazed ham, pork ribs, and squash pies. Maple syrup also makes a distinctive candy.

# MELONS

What do a honeydew melon, a Hubbard squash, and a cucumber have in common? Despite their different culinary associations, all belong to the gourd family. Most melons resemble winter squash, with thick outer flesh and cavities filled with seeds, while those big lugs, the watermelons, look surprisingly like their petite cousins, the cucumbers.

## VARIETIES

Melons come in a number of varieties, many of which are occasionally available at Greenmarket. However, the one melon that consistently grows well in this region is cantaloupe, which is available from late summer to early October. Cantaloupe, often called muskmelon, has rough, beige skin, and bright orange, sweet flesh, which is highly nutritious with lots of beta carotene.

## SELECTING

Melons should be evenly shaped and free of discoloration, cracks, or soft spots. Make sure cantaloupe is golden, not green, under the "netting," and the stem end is slightly indented. If melons are fragrant, they should be sweet and fruity (some melons have no fragrance). Melons do not continue to ripen off the vine, therefore, the larger the melon, the sweeter it will be.

## STORING

Melons can be stored, uncut, at room temperature for two or three days. Although they will not ripen, they will become softer and more succulent over time. Cut melons should be refrigerated, wrapped in plastic, and used within two days.

## PUTTING UP

Melon flesh can be frozen; remove seeds, cut the flesh into chunks or balls, pack the chunks snugly into a freezer container, and freeze. They can also be frozen in a sugar syrup. Cantaloupe and watermelon rinds can be pickled.

## PREPARING

Simply cut the melon in half with a large knife, scoop out the seeds, and cut the flesh into wedges, slices, cubes, or balls.

## SERVING SUGGESTIONS

Melons are perfect as a breakfast fruit, a low-calorie lunch (with cottage cheese), an interesting element on a dinner plate, or a light dessert. Serve melon wedges sprinkled with lemon, chopped mint, or even chopped chives or cilantro.

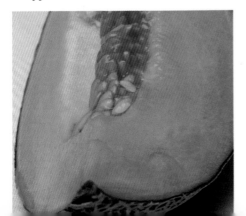

Melons combine beautifully with other fruits, including other melon varieties, berries, bananas, pineapples, and oranges, and add flavor and texture to fruit smoothies. Melons go well with fish and meat, pairing nicely with shrimp, tuna, chicken salad, and, of course, Italian prosciutto.

---

### LARS'S TROPICAL SMOOTHIE
#### Makes about 3 cups

*This recipe, created by smoothie expert Lars White, makes a delicious breakfast or a refreshing pick-me-up after exercising.*

- ¼ cantaloupe, seeded and cubed
- ½ mango, peeled, pitted, and sliced
- 1½ cups white grapes, picked over and washed
- 1 cup sliced fresh strawberries
- 1 cup pineapple chunks
- 1 small banana or 3 turbanas, peeled and cut into chunks
- ¾ cup crushed ice

Place all the ingredients in the container of a blender and blend until smooth, about 30 seconds. Serve immediately.

---

Milk is not only the basis for all other dairy products, but it is also one of nature's so-called perfect foods, being rich in protein, calcium, and a host of vitamins and minerals. Cow's milk is the most popular animal milk consumed, but goats and sheep (not to mention reindeer, buffalo, and llamas) also provide milk for human consumption.

## VARIETIES

A handful of dairy farmers sell at Greenmarket, and most of them specialize in cheese. However, two or three dairies sell milk at Greenmarket. The dairies also offer butter, yogurt, crème fraîche, and other milk products.

## Milk

**MILK.** Whole milk, low-fat milk, and skim milk are for sale. Some dairies offer milk flavored with chocolate and/or coffee. Eggnog is sometimes for sale during the holiday season.

**BUTTERMILK.** Originally a by-product of making butter, today buttermilk is made by adding special bacteria to nonfat or low-fat milk that gives it a thickened texture and tangy flavor. Some people find buttermilk too strong for drinking, but it is delicious used in many cooked or baked dishes.

**CREAM.** Cream is the fatty layer that rises to the top of nonhomogenized milk. Health-conscious people try to avoid cream, but it adds a special richness and flavor to cooked dishes. Several varieties of cream are sold: heavy, light, and half-and-half (half cream, half milk).

## Dairy Products

Some of the other dairy products that can be found at Greenmarket include:

**BUTTER.** In addition to farm-fresh butter, butters flavored with garlic, cinnamon, maple syrup, honey, and herbs are available. Use flavored butters for cooking. They're also delicious on toast or muffins.

**CHEESE.** One of the most important products of milk. (For more information, see Cheese, page 80.)

**CRÈME ANGLAISE.** A thickened sweet cream with a rich, custardy flavor and texture, crème anglaise is delicious served warm over fruit or pastry as a dessert.

**CRÈME FRAÎCHE.** A cultured cream with a tangy flavor and velvety texture (sort of a cross between yogurt and sour cream), crème fraîche can be served over a range of foods, from baked potatoes to fruit, puddings, and cakes. It can also be used to thicken sauces and dressings.

**FROMAGE BLANC.** A soft, mild-flavored white cheese, rather like cream cheese, it is sometimes available flavored with garlic or herbs. It can be served with fruit, quick breads, or bagels. It also can be used to thicken sauces.

**ICE CREAM.** Made from milk and/or cream, farm-fresh ice cream has an especially creamy consistency and a uniquely rich flavor. It comes in vanilla, chocolate, raspberry, strawberry, coffee, mint, cherry, and other flavors.

**SOUR CREAM.** Made by souring milk or cream with a lactic acid bacteria, sour cream can be used in cooking to add flavor and texture to sauces and dressings.

**YOGURT.** Several types of yogurt are available: sheep's, goat's, and cow's milk; skim and whole milk; flavored and unflavored. Yogurt can be eaten plain, with fruit, or used to thicken and flavor sauces.

## SELECTING

Check for a fresh-looking product without any indication of mold. It should smell fresh or appropriate to its type.

## STORING

Refrigerate milk and any other dairy products as soon as possible. Milk absorbs flavors readily, so keep milk bottles tightly closed in the refrigerator. Use milk or cream within five days. Other dairy products will keep from seven to 14 days, depending on type.

## PUTTING UP

Whole milk and cream can be frozen; when thawed, use for cooking, not drinking. Butter can be frozen in small (1/4-pound) quantities. Dairy products should be frozen for up to three months; thaw them in the refrigerator.

### OSOFSKY JAVA FRIBBLE
**Makes 2 fribbles**

*A member of the Osofsky family created this milk shake. Try it with Ronnybrook products.*

> 2 cups skim milk
> 3/4 cup brewed espresso or
>    dark-roast coffee
> 2 teaspoons granulated sugar
> 1/4 cup chocolate syrup

Fill an ice cube tray with the milk and freeze solid. Chill the coffee in the refrigerator. Place half the frozen milk cubes in the container of a blender, add half the coffee and 1 teaspoon of the sugar, and blend until smooth. Add 2 tablespoons (half) of the syrup and blend for about 30 seconds. Pour into a glass. Repeat with remaining ingredients for second fribble.

## SERVING SUGGESTIONS

Milk can be flavored with chocolate, honey, maple syrup, or cinnamon. Milk can be added to pureed fruit (smoothies) or vegetables (creamed soups). Vegetables, potatoes, and fruit can be topped with dairy products like yogurt, sour cream, or crème fraîche.

○ ● ○ ○
W S S F

# THE OSOFSKY FAMILY

**RONNYBROOK FARM DAIRY • Columbia County**
**Ancramdale, New York 12503**
**Stand at Union Square (Manhattan)**

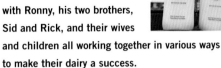

**B**est-known as the dairy that bottles its milk in glass, Ronnybrook Farm is the last of the old-fashioned dairies. Nevertheless, through smart marketing, the Osofskys have turned plain old cow's milk into a gourmet commodity. Still, those glass bottles are not just a gimmick. They are symbolic of the family's commitment to preserving the environment.

Ronnybrook has been a working dairy since 1941, when David Osofsky, from nearby Amenia, New York, established the farm with his wife, Helen, and named it for their firstborn son, Ronny. Today, more than 50 years later, the Osofsky farm remains a family-run business,

with Ronny, his two brothers, Sid and Rick, and their wives and children all working together in various ways to make their dairy a success.

Ronnybrook Farm has a herd of 140 holsteins, each of whom is named and much loved. (The much revered matriarchs are Marsha and Pauline.) Their milk, which flows from cow to market in less than three days, is fresh, sweet, and, because it comes from a single herd, distinctive. What's more, it is pasteurized, homogenized, and bottled right at the farm. (They homogenize in the old-fashioned way, too; the cream rises to the top.)

The Osofskys have been coming to Greenmarket for almost a decade. In addition to milk, they sell eggnog, butter, crème fraîche, yogurt, buttermilk, ricotta, and fromage blanc.

Third-generation cousins Gregg and Daniel Osofsky have joined the business. Although only a handful of dairy farms survive where 50 flourished less than a generation ago, Ronnybrook undoubtedly will continue to thrive.

# MUSHROOMS

Mushrooms are one of the world's most elegant vegetables. They are beautiful to look at, flavorful in unusual ways, and yet they combine beautifully with many other vegetables, much the way carrots, celery, onions, and tomatoes do. Somehow, however, we never take mushrooms for granted.

## VARIETIES

There are thousands of mushroom varieties, but only a few are cultivated in this region.

**BUTTON (OR WHITE).** The plain, white, all-purpose mushroom most commonly used for cooking.

**CREMINI (OR BROWN).** Pale beige when they are young, these gradually turn darker; a mild, all-purpose mushroom.

**HEN OF THE WOODS.** An exotic mushroom that ranges in size from as small as a Brussels sprout to as large as a cauliflower. It can look feathery and have a woodsy flavor.

**PORCINI (OR CÈPES).** A native of Italy, this is the "gourmet" mushroom, the one often considered to have the best flavor.

**PORTOBELLO.** Giant creminis 4- to 5-inches in diameter, beige in color, with a mild flavor and a thick, hearty texture.

**SHITAKE.** A native of Japan, these are umbrella-shaped, with brown-black coloring and a rich, woodsy flavor.

**WILD.** Many growers are interested in gathering wild mushrooms, and at unexpected moments may have unusual varieties to sell.

## SELECTING

Hunting for mushrooms is practically an art form. It takes very special skills and much experience to select tasty and non-poisonous mushrooms in the field. However, at Greenmarket, all that work has been done for you. Normally, only a few varieties are available, and they have been grown.

Choose firm, white, fresh-looking mushrooms, with caps closed around stems. They should be plump, spongy, and

*Button*　　　　*Cremini*

*Portobello*

*Shitake*　　　　*Hen of the woods*

clean. Avoid mushrooms that are dark-colored, or are soft or withered.

## STORING

Wipe off mushrooms with a soft paper towel or damp cloth as soon as you get home. Store mushrooms in the refrigerator, in a shallow bowl or plate covered with a damp cloth or paper towel to help keep the mushrooms from drying out. Fresh mushrooms should keep for three days.

## PUTTING UP

Raw mushrooms can be frozen whole, sliced, or minced. Wipe them off with a damp cloth, place them in an airtight container or plastic freezer bag, and freeze. Mushrooms can also be sliced, sautéed in butter, and then frozen as a sauce. Use frozen mushrooms within two months. Mushrooms can be preserved in oil or dried in a conventional oven.

## PREPARING

Avoid rinsing fungi under running water because they tend to absorb moisture easily, and then discolor, bruise, and lose their flavor. Some people discard the stems, but you can simply trim them.

## ISABELLE ALLENDE'S
## RECONCILIATION SOUP
### Serves 2

*This recipe is based on a sensuous soup from Isabelle Allende's book* Aphrodite: A Memoir of the Senses.

- ½ cup chopped portobello mushrooms (if dried, ¼ cup)
- ½ cup chopped porcini mushrooms (if dried, ¼ cup)
- ½ cup red wine
- 3 tablespoons olive oil
- 1 clove garlic
- 1 cup chopped cremini mushrooms
- 2 cups stock (beef, chicken, or vegetable)
- ¼ cup port
- Salt and freshly ground pepper
- 2 tablespoons sour cream

If using dried mushrooms, soak them in the red wine until they become plump.

Heat the olive oil in a large pot over medium heat. Add the garlic and all the mushrooms and sauté for about 5 minutes. Add the red wine and heat, stirring constantly, for about 5 minutes. Add the stock and port, season with salt and pepper to taste, and cook, covered, over low heat until the mushrooms are very soft, about 30 minutes.

Transfer the soup to a blender, working in batches to prevent the hot soup from splattering, and blend until smooth and slightly thick. Serve in warmed bowls, garnished with a dollop of sour cream.

---

Mushrooms can be blanched, sautéed, baked, broiled, and steamed. They can be cooked alone or with other vegetables.

## SERVING SUGGESTIONS

Mushrooms can be served as appetizers, soups (creamed or clear), main dishes, pasta dishes (as stuffing or a sauce), side dishes, or salads (raw or cooked). Mushrooms combine beautifully with meats and other vegetables, and can provide a savory flavor to salads, other vegetable soups, stews, casseroles, quiches, omelettes, frittatas, and potpies. They also add flavor and texture to stuffings for poultry and game birds, gravies, and sauces.

# FRANK & ANN BULICH

BULICH'S CREEKSIDE FARM • Greene County • Catskill, New York 12414
Stands at Union Square (Manhattan); and Grand Army Plaza (Brooklyn)

Like so many other Hudson Valley crops, cultivated mushrooms were a booming business less than a generation ago, although today only two farmers in the area are still growing them. Fortunately for Greenmarket, one of them is Frank Bulich, who, together with his wife, Ann, runs the Bulich Mushroom Company in Catskill, New York.

Despite what city slickers might imagine, mushrooms do not grow in fields. (The other fact that many people may not know is that giant portobello mushrooms are just overgrown creminis.) Instead, cultivated mushrooms are grown in dark "growing rooms," where the carefully controlled climate is musty, warm, and dark.

Mushroom pickers wear miner's hats with lights attached so that they can see what they are doing.

At the Bulich farm, Frank and Ann run three large growing barns, each one out fitted with rack after rack of baby mushrooms in various stages of development, nestled in moist, black, loamy soil. Each growing cycle is two to three months, depending on the variety of mushroom.

The Buliches sell their mushrooms both wholesale and retail (through Greenmarket and other local farmers markets). At various times, a few of their six children have been involved in the business. Their daughter, Bernadette, ran their Greenmarket stand at Union Square for many years, until she married Walter Kowalski and started her own flower business.

Mushroom farming is going through change at the moment. Over the past decade, as consumers have become more sophisticated about food, fascination with mushrooms has grown. With their exquisite mushrooms, Frank and Ann Bulich are poised to meet the demand.

# NECTARINES

number of hybrids, are more closely related today than they were originally. As the name (probably a derivative of *nektar,* the Greek word for "liquor of the gods") implies, nectarines are even sweeter than their peach cousins.

## SELECTING

Like many sugary fruits, nectarines will not ripen off the vine, so you must buy them ripe. Select those with a uniform shape and a slight give in texture, although they should not be too soft. Look for a golden yellow color with a rosy blush, and avoid selecting those that are very hard or slightly green, which indicates that they are not fully ripe. Avoid nectarines with bruises (tannish or brown marks) or wrinkles. Nectarines should have a fresh perfume.

## STORING

If you have purchased firm nectarines, leave them at room temperature in a paper bag for two to three days, and they will get softer and more succulent. (To speed up the process, put an apple in the bag with the nectarines.) If they are slightly soft to the touch, store them in the refrigerator crisper; they will keep for about five days.

Nectarines are basically peaches without the fuzz. Botanically, they are closely related to peaches, and, given the

## PUTTING UP

Nectarines can be frozen and preserved exactly like peaches and apricots, or in combination with them. (See "Putting Up," Peaches, page 182.)

## PREPARING

If you want to eat nectarines out of hand, simply wash them carefully in cool water. However, if you wish to peel them, blanch them for about ten seconds in boiling water; then, using a sharp knife, gently peel away the skin. To prevent cut nectarines from turning brown during preparation, sprinkle them with lemon juice.

## SERVING SUGGESTIONS

Nectarines can be used in any dish that calls for peaches or apricots. (See "Serving Suggestions," Peaches, page 183.)

---

### FRESH NECTARINE SALSA
#### Makes about 3 cups

*Serve as an accompaniment to Mexican or Tex-Mex dishes, barbecued beef or pork, grilled chicken or fish, or simply as a dip for tacos.*

>  2 cups fresh nectarines, peeled and chopped
> 1/4 cup chopped onion
> 1/2 cup finely chopped bell peppers (preferably red)
>  3 tablespoons finely chopped, seeded, fresh jalapeño peppers
> 1/4 cup lime juice (or juice from 2 limes)
>  1 garlic clove, minced
>  1 tablespoon chopped fresh cilantro
>  1 teaspoon sugar

In a medium nonreactive mixing bowl, stir together nectarines, onion, peppers, lime juice, garlic, cilantro, and sugar. Cover and chill for 1 to 2 hours before serving.

---

# OKRA

kra is a very popular vegetable in the American South and is one of the defining flavors in gumbo, the Cajun dish with which it is most closely associated. Okra is sometimes erroneously called gumbo, which is its African name. Its gummy texture adds to the thickening and texture of gumbo and other soups. It's a funny-looking, elongated seedpod that can become a bit tough and slimy as it ages. Still, it's a great pleasure to have okra as part of the New York regional harvest.

## SELECTING

Choose young, small, bright green, tender but crispy pods, about 3 inches long or less. Avoid large, overly mature okra, especially if it appears dry, grayish, limp, or tough.

## STORING

Store the okra, unwashed, in a perforated plastic bag in the refrigerator. It will remain fresh for seven to ten days.

## PUTTING UP

Okra does not can well; it can be frozen, but freezes best as part of a gumbo or soup base. It can also be pickled.

*St. Mark's Greenmarket in the East Village*

## PREPARING

Okra should be washed carefully in cold water and any stems and leaves removed. Given its strong flavor and unusual texture, okra benefits from a very brief blanching, usually for one to three minutes, before it is cooked. If pods are small, they can be cooked whole; if they are large, they should be sliced. Do not overcook them; they are tastier and less gummy when crisp. Okra can be steamed, boiled, sautéed, or deep-fried in batter.

## SERVING SUGGESTIONS

Okra can be served as a side dish or appetizer, plain, with lemon butter, a simple vinaigrette, or—as in the South—a hot sauce. Okra combines particularly well with tomatoes and corn. It can also be battered and deep-fat fried. It can be used in soups and stews, including, of course, gumbos of virtually any kind, from shrimp to chicken to lamb.

---

### CAJUN-STYLE FRIED OKRA
#### Serves 4

½ pound okra
2 cups vegetable shortening
1 egg, beaten
1 cup cornmeal mixed with
  1 teaspoon cayenne pepper
  Salt and freshly ground pepper
  Tabasco or hot sauce

---

Clean and trim the okra carefully. Melt the shortening and heat over high heat until bubbling. Dip the okra in the egg and roll it in cornmeal. Fry until the okra turns golden. Drain, add salt and pepper to taste, and serve with hot sauce.

# ONIONS

*An assortment of onions*

Like carrots and garlic, onions are a common seasoning in many recipes, serving as the substructure of flavor and aroma in cuisines throughout the world. Nevertheless, they are important vegetables in their own right. Onions are cousins to many other vegetables, including chives, leeks, scallions, and shallots. Onions and their relatives can be used interchangeably with interesting results.

## VARIETIES

As with most vegetables, scores of varieties of onion have been bred throughout the world. Two popular varieties, Bermuda and Vidalia, thrive only in warmer climates. Greenmarket offers the following:

**GOURMET ONIONS.** Very young yellow globe or red onions that have a softer, less intrusive flavor.

**PEARL ONIONS.** Small onions with a mild flavor; the best for creamed onions.

**RED ONIONS.** A large, sweet, juicy onion that is reddish purple in color.

**SCALLIONS.** Immature, green, onions. For more detailed information about scallions, see page 216.

**SHALLOTS.** Formed rather like garlic, with cloves that can be separated, shallots taste like a cross between a mild, sweet onion and garlic. They can substituted for onions in virtually any recipe, or can be prepared as a side dish on their own.

**YELLOW GLOBE ONIONS.** The standard, medium-sized, pale yellow cooking onion.

**WHITE ONIONS.** White onions can be globe-shaped or slightly elliptical. They are usually very sweet.

## SELECTING

Choose onions according to need. For example, if you need onions for flavoring, choose a basic yellow globe. If you are serving onions raw, select a red. For onion soups or creamed onions, choose white or pearl onions.

Choose onions that are firm and heavy for their size. The outer skin should be dry (no sign of moistness) and papery. Avoid onions that have green shoots or black spots, or that seem bruised or soft.

## STORING

Store onions in a cool, dry place, away from other foods. Onions should not be stored in the refrigerator. They will keep for about eight weeks. If you use part of the onion, wrap the unused section in plastic wrap and use it within three days.

## PUTTING UP

Onions will keep for several months in cold storage. They tend to turn brown and flabby when canned. Chopped onions can be frozen for use later in cooked dishes.

## PREPARING

Onions are notorious for the preparation problems they present. First, they are temperamental about having their papery skins removed. (Slice off the top and bottom of the onion and slide off the skin. If the onions are young, you may need to blanch them for one minute to help loosen their skins.)

Onions are famous for causing tearing. Many old wives' tales advise on how to avoid this problem, but the quickest solution is to just chop and bear it. Onions can be baked, boiled, braised, sautéed, and cooked in a microwave oven. When cooked, they often have a strong aroma that to most people is appealing, if not mouthwatering.

## SERVING SUGGESTIONS

Onions and their relatives are delicious served raw in salads (minced, chopped, or sliced into rings), or thinly sliced on sandwiches. Onions can be used to season stews, sauces, casseroles, soups, even alcoholic drinks. On their own, they can be served as a side dish (creamed, sautéed, or French fried), a soup (cream of onion; French onion), or a savory main dish (stuffed and baked).

*A young gourmet onion*

## SARAH'S CREAMED ONIONS
### Serves 4 to 6

*My grandmother was an elegant cook, and always made these creamed onions for family dinners during the holidays.*

24 small white onions, papery skins removed
3 tablespoons butter
3 tablespoons flour
1½ cups light cream
1 teaspoon ground cloves
2 teaspoons ground nutmeg
¼ cup chopped chives
½ teaspoon white pepper
Salt
2 tablespoons chopped parsley

Place the onions in a large saucepan. Add enough cold, salted water to just cover them and bring to a boil. Reduce the heat and simmer until the onions are tender, about 30 minutes. Drain.

In a large, nonreactive saucepan, melt the butter over low heat. Add the flour a little bit at a time, stirring or whisking constantly, until blended. Stir in the cream and continue cooking, stirring constantly, until the sauce thickens and is smooth. (If the sauce is too thick for your taste, add more cream or a tablespoon or two of whole milk.)

Stir in the cloves, nutmeg, chives, white pepper, and salt to taste. Gently fold in the onions and warm through. Serve hot, garnished with chopped parsley.

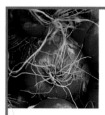

## ALEX PAFFENROTH

PAFFENROTH FARM • Orange County • Warwick, New York 10990
Stand at Union Square (Manhattan)

As you drive up Little York Road toward Alex Paffenroth's farm, you pass several comfortable, suburban-looking houses. You sense that you are near farmland, but you could just as easily be on a suburban street. It isn't until you turn into Alex's driveway that you catch a glimpse of the incredibly rich "black dirt" that makes up the beautiful 65-acre Paffenroth farm in the heart of Orange County.

Alex Paffenroth's land has been in his family for four generations. For most of that time, the primary crop was onions. In fact, the "Black Dirt" region was once known as the "Onion Capital of the World," not only because a large percentage of the nation's onion crop came from this area, but because onions grew so easily in this loamy soil.

Like so many other growers in the New York region, Alex felt the impact of the presence of large Western growers on his wholesale business. Then, about 15 years ago, Alex's crop was virtually wiped out in a matter of minutes in a freak hailstorm. At that moment, Alex decided to diversify. He also decided that he could very possibly make more money selling directly to consumers through New York's Greenmarket than continuing to sell wholesale and competing with the huge growers.

Today, Alex plays host to one of the most abundant and diverse stands at Greenmarket. He still sells lots of varieties of onion, and its relations, including scallions, leeks, chives, and shallots. But he also features an array of radishes, many varieties of summer and winter squash, cauliflower, celery, celery root, carrots, garlic, a broad range of herbs, lettuces, greens, and sprouts.

Alex seems to be a shy man, but his eyes sparkle when he talks about his farm and his crops. If you have questions about any of his produce, he'll be delighted to talk to you about it.

# PARSNIPS

Colonial New Englanders ate parsnips in much the same way we eat potatoes. Parsnips are close cousins to carrots; they not only look like white carrots, they have the same sort of sweetness. Pilgrims and Brahmins alike frequently downed parsnips prepared in a variety of ways, including boiled, steamed, mashed, and fried. Parsnips have fallen out of favor, but are well worth a fresh look.

## SELECTING

Choose small- to medium-sized roots that are firm to the touch. Avoid roots that are rubbery or too spotted.

## STORING

Store parsnips in a cool bin or in the vegetable crisper of the refrigerator. Don't wash them until you are ready to cook them. They will last in the refrigerator for at least two weeks, and probably longer.

## PUTTING UP

Some sources suggest that the best way to preserve parsnips is to leave them in the ground covered with a thin coating of mulch. The next-best preservation method for parsnips is root-cellaring. Parsnips are stored by many farmers in precisely this way, and thus are available at Greenmarket all winter.

Parsnips can also be canned (using the hot-pack method). Or they may be frozen; to freeze, parsnips should first be chopped, sliced, or puréed.

## PREPARING

Trim the green tops and the tapering roots. Scrub the parsnips, and peel them with a vegetable peeler as you would carrots. Cut larger roots into quarters and remove any woody, then core. Cut lengthwise into thick slices.

Cook parsnips by steaming them, boiling them in salted water, or roasting them. Season steamed parsnips with butter and cinnamon or nutmeg to bring out the root's natural sweetness. Or, if you are watching calories, garnish lightly with freshly chopped parsley, chives, or tarragon.

## SERVING SUGGESTIONS

Blessed with a peppery, sweet taste, parsnips can be served as an ideal accompaniment to strong-flavored meats, particularly beef, lamb, pork, game birds, or strong fish. Traditionally, parsnips were always served with boiled beef or salted cod.

A steaming bowl of julienned parsnips and carrots is one of the prettiest side dishes, especially on a traditional Thanksgiving table. Parsnips are delicious mashed or pureed, either alone or mixed with potatoes. Sliced parsnips make a nice addition to soups and stews.

### PARSNIP PUREE
#### Serves 6

- 2 pounds parsnips
- 2 tablespoons butter
- 1 egg yolk
- 1 tablespoon honey
- 1 teaspoon ground cinnamon
- 1 teaspoon ground nutmeg
  Salt and freshly ground pepper

Trim the tops and roots from the parsnips. Peel and cut them crosswise into thick slices. In a pan of salted water, cover and simmer for about 20 minutes, or until tender.

Drain the parsnips and mash them or put them through a food mill. Return them to the pan, add the butter, and beat until fluffy. Beat in the egg yolk, honey, cinnamon, and nutmeg. Season with salt and pepper to taste.

# PEACHES

The best thing about the peaches you buy at Greenmarket is that they have been bred for sweetness, not durability. (With peaches, you can't have both.) Peaches begin to show up in mid-summer, but it's not until late August that peaches become succulent and sweet.

## SELECTING

Peaches fall into two groups: freestones and clingstones. Freestones are better for eating out of hand because the flesh does not stick to the stone, while clingstones are better for canning because the fruit holds its shape.

Peaches do not ripen off the vine, so buy them ripe. Select medium- to large-sized peaches with a uniform shape and a slight give. Look for a golden color (a pink blush has to do with variety, not ripeness). Avoid those with bruises or wrinkles.

## STORING

Although peaches will not ripen or sweeten, once off the vine, they will get softer. If you have purchased firm peaches, leave them at room temperature in a paper bag for two or three days. When soft, store them in the refrigerator crisper; they will keep for about five days.

## PUTTING UP

Peaches are delicious canned, especially with brandy or aged bourbon. Peaches can also be preserved as peach butter, jelly, or jam; or frozen in syrup, sugar, or plain. Peaches can also be dried.

## PREPARING

If you want to eat peaches out of hand, simply wash them carefully in cool water. (The fuzzy skin is part of the joy of eating a peach.) For easier peeling, blanch them for about ten seconds in boiling water, then peel. To prevent cut peaches from turning brown, sprinkle them with lemon juice. Fresh peaches can be served raw, baked, grilled, broiled, or poached.

## SERVING SUGGESTIONS

Peaches are delicious eaten out of hand or sliced and served with confectioners' sugar, cream, ice cream, or yogurt, or over cereal. They make a nice accompaniment to roast chicken, duck, pork, and ham, either made into a sauce or served halved and grilled with cinnamon and brown sugar. Being naturally sweet, peaches can be used to flavor, or as the main ingrdient in, quick breads, pies, cakes, cobblers, puddings, and other desserts.

---

### UNION SQUARE CAFE
### PEACH & BLUEBERRY COBBLER
**Serves 4 to 6**

*Michael Romano, the chef at the famed Union Square Cafe, created this version of a classic dessert.*

  2  cups blueberries, cleaned
  2  pounds fresh peaches, peeled, pitted, and sliced (about 7 cups)
  ½  teaspoon ground cardamom
  ½  teaspoon grated lemon zest
  5  tablespoons sugar
  2  cups plus 1 tablespoon cake flour
  1  tablespoon baking powder
    Pinch of salt
  5  tablespoons unsalted butter, cut into bits
  ¾  cup plus 1 tablespoon heavy cream

Preheat the oven to 400°F. Combine the blueberries and peaches with the cardamom, lemon zest, 2 tablespoons of the sugar, and 1 tablespoon of the flour, then transfer to a deep, ovenproof dish.

To make the pastry, sift the 2 cups of flour, the remaining sugar, the baking powder, and salt into a large bowl. Using two butter knives, combine the butter and flour mixture, then stir in ¾ cup cream to make a soft dough. Turn the dough out onto a work surface and roll out to ¾-inch thickness. With a biscuit cutter, cut out 3-inch rounds. Arrange the rounds atop the fruit and brush with 1 tablespoon heavy cream. Bake for 30 minutes, until bubbly and lightly browned. Serve warm.

# PEARS

*Bosc pears*

I n the United States, pears have never enjoyed the popularity of apples, peaches, or berries, whereas in France and Italy, pears are among the most popular fruits.

Most pears grown commercially in the United States come from the Pacific Coast. Nevertheless, several regional farmers grow pears, which are available at Greenmarket from late August through October.

## VARIETIES

**ANJOU.** A green, oval-shaped pear with white, rather bland-tasting flesh; a good all-purpose pear.

**BARTLETT.** A large, juicy, yellow-green (with a pink blush) pear; good for canning.

**BOSC.** A firm, long-necked, reddish brown pear; holds its shape well when baked or poached.

**COMICE.** Green-skinned, sweet, and flavorful; a good dessert pear.

**SECKEL.** A tiny, very sweet pear.

## SELECTING

Pears should be smooth and relatively blemish free. Unlike many other fruits, pears continue to ripen after they have been picked, and those at Greenmarket may not yet be their characteristic color, and will

*Seckel pears*

usually require a bit more ripening. Unless you will be preparing them immediately, select firm pears and allow them to ripen at room temperature in your kitchen.

## STORING

Store pears at room temperature until they are ripe; refrigerate ripe fruit in the crisper. (You can keep unripe fruit in the refrigerator, but the cool air will inhibit the ripening process.) To speed ripening, place the fruit in a paper bag. Never store pears in an unperforated plastic bag; the lack of oxygen will cause them to rot quickly.

## PUTTING UP

Bartlett pears, because of their size and succulence, are the best pears to put up. Pears can well using the hot-pack method. Pears make delicious jams, jellies, conserves, butters, chutneys, juice, nectar, and cider. Pears can be frozen in syrup or as a puree; they also can be dried.

## PREPARING

For many recipes, pears need not be peeled. However, for those recipes that require them to be peeled, place the peeled slices in acidulated water (with lemon juice or white vinegar) so they don't turn brown.

## SERVING SUGGESTIONS

Pears can be eaten raw, out of hand or served with a good cheese. They can be poached, roasted, sautéed, and baked. Serve chopped pears over cereal, ice cream, or in yogurt. Add to batter for muffins, pancakes, waffles, and other quick breads. Bake pears in pies, tarts, cakes, or cookies. Pears combine well with other fruits, particularly apples and raisins. They also accept flavorings well, particularly cinnamon, nutmeg, and ginger.

*Bartlett pears*

# PEAS

Peas conjure up a vision of a farmer's wife, sitting in a rocking chair on a late afternoon in summer, shelling garden peas for dinner. Since peas were one of the first vegetables to be commercially canned in the 1860s, the farmer's wife probably welcomed the time she saved preparing dinner. Still, bland, gray-green canned peas bore no resemblance to freshly picked peas, and that remains true today.

Thanks to Greenmarket, we can now revel in the flavor of fresh peas. They begin to arrive in late June and are available throughout the summer.

*Sugar snap peas*

## VARIETIES

A number of varieties of pea are available in this region:

**GARDEN PEAS (OR ENGLISH PEAS)** are the traditional round, green peas we have eaten since infancy. They must be removed from their tough pods before they can be cooked and eaten.

**SNOW PEAS (OR CHINESE SNOW PEAS)**

are bred to be eaten whole, pod and all. They are a bright, pale green, elegantly thin (almost translucent), and very crisp. Snow peas are a very popular vegetable in Chinese cooking.

**SUGAR SNAP PEAS (OR SUGAR PEAS),** a cross between English peas and snow peas, are dainty and sweet. Although smaller, they are the same color and texture as garden peas, but their pods are so delicate they can be eaten whole, like snow peas. They are very popular at Greenmarket.

## SELECTING

Look for peas that have clear, green pods that show no signs of blemishes or shriveling. The peas should feel firm inside their pods.

## STORING

Peas begin to lose their sweetness the moment they are picked. Therefore, store them, unwashed, in a plastic bag in the refrigerator for no more than two or three days. Don't shell garden peas until just before preparing them.

## PUTTING UP

Peas are one of the easiest vegetables to freeze, can, and dry. Garden peas, commercially frozen, canned, or dried, are readily available and inexpensive, so it's hardly worth the effort or expense to preserve them yourself. However, sugar snap and snow peas are worth freezing. Trim them, blanch them for one minute, drain, then pack them in an airtight container or a freezer bag. They will keep for six months.

## PREPARING

To shell garden peas, break off the stem, "string" the pod down the side, and pop

*Garden peas*

open the seam. Gently nudge the peas out of the pods with your finger. Save the pods for making vegetable stock; they add a piquant flavor to the stock. If you can't make stock immediately, freeze them in a plastic freezer container until needed.

Before cooking snow peas and sugar snaps, trim the ends and rinse them gently.

## SERVING SUGGESTIONS

To cook fresh peas, steam them in lightly salted water, and serve, lightly buttered or plain, with a sprinkling of chopped fresh mint, tarragon, or dill.

Peas make an ideal addition to soups, stews, casseroles, pasta sauces, risottos, and stir-fries. Peas of all kinds can be added raw or barely blanched to salads, or served as an hors d'oeuvre or crudité.

# PEPPERS

Sweet peppers have long been a staple crop of this region, and, in recent years, hot peppers have become more popular. Several farmers, including Ted Blew of Oak Grove Plantation and Tim Stark of Eckerton Hill Farm have grown scores of varieties, and a number of Greenmarket customers have become connoisseurs.

*A variety of hot peppers*

## VARIETIES

Literally hundreds of varieties of sweet and hot peppers exist, and many are available at Greenmarket, including:

### Sweet Peppers

**BANANA.** A mild yellow pepper that looks like a Hungarian wax, but is not nearly as hot.

**BELL PEPPERS.** These can be green, red, yellow, orange, and even brown or purple,

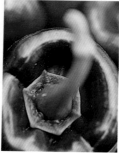

*Bell pepper*      *Bell pepper*

depending upon the variety and the stage of maturity. As they ripen on the vine, they change color. Green peppers are mature, but not fully ripe, whereas red peppers are fully ripened and therefore sweeter. The yellow and orange bell peppers are between the green and red.

## Hot Peppers (Chilies)

**ANCHO.** Poblano peppers after drying; sweet, fruity, relatively mild.

**ANAHEIM.** A mild to medium-hot pepper. Delicious fresh, roasted, and in sauces.

**CAYENNE.** One of the hottest peppers, it is good in gumbos, creoles, and fish dishes.

**HABAÑERO.** An extremely hot, aromatic pepper with an apricot-like flavor.

**HUNGARIAN WAX.** A medium-hot pepper that is delicious raw or cooked.

**JALAPEÑO.** The most popular hot pepper, it is very hot, but not as hot as a habañero or a serrano.

**MEXI-BELL.** A cross between a miniature bell pepper and a hot pepper, with some bite to it.

**PETER PEPPER.** An extremely hot pepper. Excellent dried.

**POBLANO.** Medium-hot Mexican peppers, these are ancho peppers in the green state, and look like small, elongated, sweet bell peppers.

**SCOTCH BONNET.** A superhot pepper that comes in red, yellow, and brown.

**SERRANO.** A superhot pepper used in chili, hot, and dried.

*Hungarian wax peppers*

## SELECTING

All peppers, sweet or hot, should be well-shaped, firm, and relatively shiny. The skin should be smooth and the stems fresh. Bell peppers should have thick walls and feel heavy and succulent for their size.

*Habañero peppers*

## STORING

Store sweet peppers, unwashed, in a plastic bag in the refrigerator. They will keep for about a week. Wrap fresh hot peppers in paper towels or place in a perforated plastic bag and refrigerate. Hot peppers will keep for up to four weeks.

## PUTTING UP

All peppers, sweet or hot, can be canned, frozen, and dried.

## PREPARING

Wash sweet peppers just before using them. Most will need to be cored, seeded, and chopped or sliced.

The substance that makes chili peppers taste so hot (capsaicin) can also burn skin and eyes. Many experts recommend wearing thin-rubber protective gloves when working with peppers. If you don't have gloves or resist wearing them, avoid touching your face and eyes while working and wash your hands thoroughly after chopping. Peppers can be baked, blanched, roasted, and sautéed.

## SERVING SUGGESTIONS

Peppers are almost as versatile as tomatoes. They are delicious served raw, either in salads or as part of a crudités platter. They can be roasted over the flame of a gas burner or on an outdoor grill. Sweet or hot, they can be chopped and included as part of a stir-fry, a pasta, or other sauce, a salsa, or a pureed soup. Both sweet and hot peppers can be stuffed with meat, grains, or vegetable mélanges. Sweet peppers and, more particularly, hot peppers are important ingredients in Tex-Mex and Mexican cuisines.

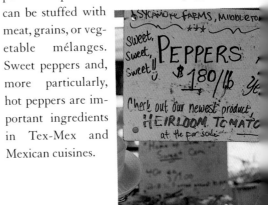

# TIM STARK

ECKERTON HILL FARM • Berks County • Lenhartsville, Pennsylvania 19526
Stand at Union Square (Manhattan)

Over the past couple of years, Tim Stark has turned into the Brad Pitt of Greenmarket. His produce has been featured on the covers of *Gourmet* and several other major food magazines, and in dishes served at some of the fanciest restaurants in town, such as Gramercy Tavern, Restaurant Daniel, Ocean, and Aureole. Tim, himself, has appeared on major television programs and in the *New York Times*. So how has Tim attained this glamour status? Peppers, that's how!

Until six years ago, Tim was a freelance writer and teacher. His mother, Sharon Sheehey Stark, also a fiction writer, owned Eckerton Hill Farm in east-central Pennsylvania, and Tim decided to try his hand at farming her land. He loved it; it hardly seemed like work to him. Before long, he became fascinated with heirloom plants, particularly tomatoes and peppers.

Today, Tim specializes in heirloom vegetables. On only 10 acres, he cultivates over 200 varieties of pepper (both sweet and hot), 150 varieties of tomato, and 30 varieties of lettuce.

He has also experimented with unusual varieties of melon and watermelon with lovely names like Orange Glow and Amish Moon and Stars.

In addition to his produce, Tim sells miniature pepper plants which can serve as interesting decorative houseplants. Also, he and his wife, Jill, sell their own hot sauce, called "Burning Love Hot Sauce," and a special hot-pepper vinegar.

Tim calls Eckerton Hill Farm the "Home of the Backyard Tomato and Chilies from Around the World." He claims that his success has made farming work for him, but you can see that he loves it. And it's all because of those peppers!

# PLUMS

*Sumptuous plums on display*

heads) are actually a type of old-fashioned sugar candy. Conversely, some foods contain—or actually are—plums, but we tend not to be aware of it. For example, we often forget that prunes are dried plums or that Chinese duck sauce is a puree of plums.

## VARIETIES

Although a few plum varieties are native to North America, most are either Japanese or European. Plums come in many colors: purple, blue, red, and greenish yellow. Most have yellow or reddish flesh.

**JAPANESE VARIETIES** tend to be juicy and sweet. They include Santa Rosa, Friar, and Kelsey (or Green Gage). Occasionally a very sweet variety called sugar plums are available.

**EUROPEAN VARIETIES** are smaller, denser, tarter, and less juicy. They include Damson, Stanley, Italian, and Empress. These are recommended for canning and baking.

## SELECTING

Plums are available from July through September. Look for plums that are plump and well colored for their variety and exude a sweet fragrance. A ripe plum will have some give, but you can buy harder plums

M any foods bear a "plum" appellation, but have little to do with plums. For example, English plum pudding is made with currants and raisins, not plums; and sugar plums (that dance in children's

and allow them to soften. Avoid plums with shriveled or broken skin or spots.

## STORING

To soften plums, store them in a paper bag at room temperature for a day or two. Then store them in the refrigerator crisper. They will keep for about five days.

## PUTTING UP

Can plums whole in syrup. Freeze plums whole or cut up for jams or pie fillings; freeze them in sugar or pureed for sauces. Drying plums requires special equipment.

## PREPARING

Wash plums gently in cool water. For most recipes you need not peel plums because the skin is soft and sweet. If you do need to peel them, blanch them briefly in boiling water and peel with a paring knife.

## SERVING SUGGESTIONS

Serve plums raw (out of hand or sliced), baked, poached, or pureed. Plums combine well with other fruits, particularly peaches, nectarines, and apricots. They also make beautiful pies and tarts. (Select several varieties and combine them in one pie.)

### SIMPLE PLUM PIE
**Makes one 9-inch pie**

*This is a simple pie to make when plums are at their most succulent.*

3 pounds firm plums, washed, pitted, and quartered
½ cup sifted all-purpose flour
½ cup granulated sugar
¼ teaspoon ground cinnamon
¼ teaspoon ground nutmeg
2 tablespoons cold, unsalted butter, cut into small pieces
Juice of ½ lemon
Confectioners' sugar
2 9-inch frozen pie shells, defrosted

Preheat the oven to 400°F. Place the fruit in a large bowl and toss with the flour, sugar, cinnamon, nutmeg, butter, and lemon juice. Mound the filling in one of the pie shells, drape the second shell over the top, and make slits in it to allow the steam to escape. Bake for about 40 minutes. Let cool, dust with confectioners' sugar, and serve.

# POTATOES

**P**erpetual dieters have a knee-jerk response to potatoes and avoid them like the plague. The fact is, a potato has no more calories than an apple of similar size. Its carbohydrates are complex, and it is chock full of vitamins and minerals. As with pasta, it's what we put on top of potatoes—oil, butter, cheese, sour cream, bacon chips, and salt—that accounts for the threat to the arteries and thighs.

Like tomatoes, potatoes are tuberous members of the nightshade family, and the edible part is actually an underground stem, not a root, as is commonly thought.

Potatoes in many varieties are perhaps the most widely cultivated and consumed vegetable in the world. They are grown across the United States, particularly in the Northwest (especially Idaho), Maine and, fortunately for Greenmarket, in New Jersey and New York.

## BASIC VARIETIES

Potatoes are differentiated in several ways: by age, shape, color, and particularly whether they are starchy or waxy. Here is an overview:

**NEW POTATOES.** Only potatoes that are freshly harvested and young can be considered new potatoes. They have very thin, delicate skin. In fact, new potatoes are often identified by their ragged skin, which is referred to as "feathered" or "skinned." New potatoes vary in size from less than 1 inch to 3 inches in diameter, and have a delicate, sweet flavor. New potatoes are available from late spring through the summer.

**FINGERLING POTATOES.** A name given to small, usually young potatoes of several varieties that are about the size and shape of a thumb.

*Fingerling potatoes*

**RUSSET POTATOES (OR IDAHO POTATOES)** are oval shaped, can weigh a pound or more each, have dark brown skin and starchy white flesh. (Starchy means that the flesh is flaky and tends to fall apart when cooked.) Russets are especially good for baking and

*Round red potatoes*

deep-fat frying. Long russet potatoes are most commonly grown in Idaho, but some farmers do cultivate them in our region.

**LONG WHITES** are all-purpose potatoes. They are medium-sized and have a pale tan skin and starchy, white flesh.

**ROUND REDS** have smooth, pinkish-red skin and waxy flesh. (Waxy flesh means that the potatoes have less starch, are moist, not flaky, and hold together after they are cooked.) They are good for boiling and roasting, and hold up well in stews and potato salads.

**ROUND WHITES** have the tan skin of long white potatoes, but are smaller and rounder. They have flesh that is more starchy than reds, less starchy than long whites. They are good all-purpose potatoes.

## SPECIAL VARIETIES

Several hundred varieties of potato, including many European and American heirloom varieties, are cultivated in the United States, and scores of those varieties are available at Greenmarket. Among the favorites are:

**BINTJE.** A firm, yellow-fleshed, butter-flavored, European heirloom; good for roasting, boiling, or frying.

**BLUE.** An heirloom variety that comes

in many shades, ranging from pale blue to dark purple. The flesh is white or cream colored. Blues are attractive looking and delicous served boiled, like a new potato.

**CARIB.** A creamy, sweet-flavored potato; good for baking, boiling, or roasting.

**CAROLA.** A creamy, butter-flavored, semi-waxy, yellow-fleshed, German heirloom; considered by some farmers to be the best of the yellows; a good all-purpose potato.

**LA RATTE (OR LA REINE).** A French fingerling with yellow flesh, a rich, buttery flavor, and waxy texture; good for boiling, roasting, or salads.

**RED NORLAND.** A white-fleshed, creamy and sweet potato; good boiled, roasted, or fried.

**RUBY CRESCENT.** A Peruvian variety; nutty-flavored; rich, creamy, yellow flesh; waxy texture; good for roasting or boiling.

**RUSSIAN YELLOW FINGERLING.** A yellow-fleshed, sweet, creamy, butter-flavored potato; excellent for boiling or roasting.

**YUKON GOLD.** A succulent, sweet, butter-flavored, yellow-fleshed potato; good all-purpose potato; the most popular of the special varieties.

## SELECTING

Choose smooth, well-shaped potatoes, free of sprouts or a greenish cast, which indicate decay and possibly the presence of solanine, a toxin. The potatoes should feel firm, not spongy; the eyes should be minimal, and the skin should be free of cracks, wrinkles, bruises, dampness, or discoloration. (The exception is new potatoes, which are often identified by their "feathered" skins.)

## STORING

Keep the potatoes, unwashed, in a brown paper bag or a perforated plastic bag, and store them in a cool, dry place. Do not store potatoes in the refrigerator. Potato starch turns to sugar if the potatoes are stored at temperatures under about 45 degrees, and gives the potatoes an unpleasant sweetish flavor. Conversely, don't store potatoes in a warm place because the heat encourages sprouting. In addition, don't store potatoes with onions; the combination of the two produces gases that destroy both.

Mature potatoes will last for two to three months or longer, depending upon condi-

tions; new potatoes are more perishable and should be eaten within a week.

## PUTTING UP

The best way to preserve potatoes is in a root cellar. Potatoes may be dried or canned using the hot-pack method, but it is hardly worth the effort, as excellent potatoes are available year-round. Uncooked potatoes don't freeze well; however, mashed potatoes, potato casseroles, or other potatos dishes can be frozen.

## PREPARING

Much of a potato's nutrition, including fiber, is in its skin, so leave the skin on whenever possible. Simply scrub the potatoes and gently remove the eyes. If you need to peel the potatoes, use a vegetable peeler and remove the thinnest layer possible. Contact with aluminum or iron will discolor some varieties of potatoes, so do not peel or cut potatoes with a carbon-steel knife, and cook them in an aluminum pot.

Potatoes can be baked, roasted, boiled, steamed, microwaved, deep-fried, and mashed. Potato dishes work better if you choose the correct variety of potato for the type of dish you are preparing.

*Greenmarket at Bowling Green*

**BAKED.** For baking potatoes, russets are the best. Two caveats: First, do not wrap them in foil. Foil does not allow moisture to escape, causing the potato to steam instead of bake and the flesh to become mushy and/or hard instead of fluffy. Second, pierce the skin in several places with a sharp knife. To allow the potato to bake quickly and evenly, use a large baking nail, a metal skewer, or even a new, clean household nail. Insert the nail lengthwise into the potato, and bake.

**BOILED OR STEAMED.** For boiled or steamed dishes, including soups and stews, use waxy potatoes, generally those of the round, red variety. If the potatoes are small, boil or steam them with their skins on; if they need to be sliced or chopped, cut them into pieces leaving the skins on if possible.

**FRIED.** Russets are the best potatoes for making French fries; fry them with or without their skins. For skillet frying, choose round whites or waxy varieties that are less likely to break down.

**MASHED.** Russets, because they are so starchy, make good mashed potatoes, although other starchy whites also work well. Classic mashed potatoes are made with peeled and boiled potatoes that are mashed with a hand masher or a ricer then combined with whole milk and butter. However, consider making mashed potatoes with skins left on (chop the potatoes before boiling them so the skin is in small pieces). Instead of milk, use skim milk, cream, sour cream, créme fraîche, or yogurt. For lighter, fluffier mashed potatoes, use more milk and less (or no) butter. Whip the potatoes with an electric mixer instead of a hand masher for a smoother texture.

**MICROWAVED.** Any variety of potato can be cooked in the microwave oven. Pierce the potatoes with a fork to prevent them from exploding, set them on a paper towel in a circular pattern, and rotate them once during the cooking process. Cooking time will depend on the size and number of potatoes being cooked.

**ROASTED.** Waxy potatoes, such as round reds and fingerlings, are better for roasting, and can be cooked with skin on. Gently scrub the potatoes, then arrange them in the roasting pan with meat or other vegetables.

## SERVING SUGGESTIONS

Who doesn't love potatoes? Mashed potatoes, particularly, are adored by everyone from infants to octogenarians. They can be

flavored in infinite ways, with cheese, onions, herbs, garlic, bacon, or green vegetables. Colcannon and Champ are classic mashed potato casseroles, and shepherd's pie, featuring mashed potatoes on top of a beef or lamb stew, is a famous English dish.

When served as a side dish, potatoes can be steamed, boiled, scalloped, fried, sautéed, or mashed in myriad ways, and then combined with any number of meats and vegetables. Classic side dishes featuring potatoes include potatoes Anna, potatoes Lyonnaise, and potatoes au gratin.

Potatoes can be served as appetizers (tiny boiled potatoes filled with mashed potatoes, sour cream, and caviar are delicious), as soups and stews (as the main ingredient, a thickener, or an additional vegetable), or as the central ingredient in curries, frittatas, croquettes, knishes, pirogies, stuffings, omelettes, and savory pies. They can also be used in breads, muffins, cakes, and pies.

# POULTRY, MEAT, & GAME

Like the difference between vine-ripened and store-bought tomatoes, the difference between a fresh-killed chicken and one purchased in the grocery store is considerable. All sorts of poultry, meats, and game are available at Greenmarket. Regardless of the type, the farmer can only sell animals he has raised from weaning. Butchering and smoking may be done off-farm.

## VARIETIES

**POULTRY.** Chicken, turkey (fresh, wild, and smoked), and Rock Cornish game hen (as well as their eggs) are sold.

**MEAT.** Beef, pork, lamb, and sausages made from these meats are sold.

**GAME.** Pheasant, duck, goose, quail, and venison are a few of the types of game birds and meats sold.

## SELECTING

The poultry, meat, or game should look fresh and have no unpleasant odor. Each type of meat is different, however. Ask the farmers about their products.

## STORING & FREEZING

Store meat, poultry, and game in the coldest part of the refrigerator. Cook it within two days. Poultry, meat, and game freeze well. Carefully wrapped in plastic and frozen, they will keep for a year.

## PREPARING & SERVING

Every type and each different cut of meat requires a different method of handling. Many need to be carefully seasoned and slowly cooked for best flavor. Consult good poultry, meat, and game cookbooks for instructions and ideas.

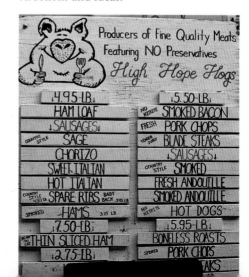

# THE QUATTROCIOCCHI FAMILY

QUATTRO'S GAME FARM • Dutchess County • Pleasant Valley, New York 12569
Stand at Union Square (Manahattan)

The Quattro's stand at the Union Square Greenmarket is endlessly fascinating. No matter what time of year, you can always find an incredible array of fascinating treats—from fresh-killed chickens, turkeys, ducks, and pheasants to smoked quail, smoked turkey, and specially prepared duck sausage.

The Quattrociocchi family farm was established in 1944 by Carmela Quattrociocchi's mother, Maria Fanelli. Maria's husband had been a dairy farmer in Millbrook. When he died at age 50, leaving Maria with eight children to raise, Maria had some tough choices to make. Maria concluded that she could not handle a dairy farm on her own, but she could, with some help from the children, raise poultry.

She started with turkeys and laying hens, specializing in fresh-killed turkeys (a perennial holiday bird) and eggs. As she became more knowledgeable, she expanded into selling additional birds, including pheasants, ducks, guinea hens, capons, geese, and wild turkeys.

Carmela was the youngest of the eight children and the only girl in her family. She met her husband, Frank, who owned a store in Poughkeepsie, when she was a teenager, but it was years before the two were allowed to marry. But marry they did, and had two sons, Sal and Frank.

The Quattrociocchis also have a retail grocery outlet located just off the Taconic State Parkway, a store some foodies believe to be one of the best sources for fresh poultry, meat, and game on the East Coast. They also smoke their own game and poultry.

The Quattrociocchi family has been coming to Greenmarket since the early 1980s, and their turkeys and other meats have earned a well-deserved reputation for being fresh, flavorful, and unique. Just one hint: Order in advance.

# PRETZELS

For generations, handmade pretzels have been the secret of the Pennsylvania Dutch. Several pretzel bakeries dotted the Pennsylvania landscape until recent years, when, due to competition from commercial producers, most handmade pretzel bakers went out of business. Still, no machine-made pretzel can match the taste of a handmade one.

## HANDMADE PRETZELS

Handmade pretzels start with a simple sour dough that contains only unbleached flour, water, salt, and yeast. No oil or shortening (which is why they are hard), sweeteners or preservatives, are added.

**TWISTING.** Hand rolling and twisting create the unique pretzel texture. (Often, on the underside of pretzels, a fingerprint can be detected where the dough tip ends have been pressed down.)

**SODA BATH.** After being twisted, the pretzels are boiled in a special baking soda bath that raises the gluten on the pretzel's surface to create the dark brown crust. Then the pretzels are salted by hand.

**DRYING.** Handmade pretzels are baked in a 500°F stone-lined oven for 15 minutes. This high temperature leaves the centers a little soft, but then the pretzels are dried in a very low-temperature oven. Drying contributes to the crunchy texture, which makes handmade pretzels fragile, but also helps preserve them.

## STORING

Store pretzels in a plastic bag or airtight canister. They will stay fresh for weeks.

## SERVING SUGGESTIONS

Pretzels are a perfect low-calorie snack. They can be served as an alternative to crackers with dips, sauces, cheeses, or mustard. For a sweet, they can be dipped in chocolate and teamed with ice cream.

W S S F

# CLARENCE MARTIN & ALFRED MILANESE

MARTIN'S HANDMADE PRETZELS • Lancaster County • Akron, Pennsylvania 17501
Stands at Union Square, I.S. 77, and City Hall (Manhattan) • Borough Hall and
Grand Army Plaza (Brooklyn)

*Twisting pretzels
in the bakery*

The Martin family has been producing handmade pretzels for more than 60 years. Henry Martin started the business in the 1930s, passed it on to his nephew, Lloyd in the 1970s, who, in turn, sold it to his brother, Clarence, the present owner.

The Martins are Mennonites, and employ family members as well as other Mennonite and Amish friends from the area to work in their bakery. A crew of 13 works ten-hour days, starting at 6 A.M. Each employee performs every task, including mixing dough, twisting, baking, and packing the pretzels. The workers sometimes sing hymns as they toil, which makes for a delightful atmosphere in the bakery.

Alfred Milanese has been Martin's Pretzels' sole distributor for more than 15 years. A native of Bethesda, Maryland, Alfred is also a writer, historian, and photographer. While living in Lancaster County in the early 1980s, Alfred became a connoisseur of homemade pretzels in general, and a devotee of Martin's Pretzels in particular.

When he moved to New York City, Alfred was convinced urban denizens would love Martin's Pretzels as much as he did, so he decided to try selling them in Manhattan, and eventually he ended up establishing one of the most popular stands at Greenmarket. But Alfred is not just a representative of Martin's Pretzels, he is a close family friend with great respect for the Martins, their work, and their beliefs.

*Alfred Milanese (left) and Clarence Martin*

# PUMPKINS

Unlike their winter squash relations, pumpkins are available for only a brief period of time at Greenmarket, from mid-September through late November. Most pumpkins, which belong to a variety known as Connecticut Field pumpkins, are not really meant for eating, but rather for decoration, primarily as jack-o'-lanterns at Halloween. Still, a few varieties, such as sugar pumpkins, are bred for cooking.

## SELECTING

Choose pumpkins that are bright orange in color and heavy for their size; the skin should be smooth and blemish free. Select pumpkins with the stem still attached, which should be smooth and dry. If you are choosing a pumpkin for a jack-o'-lantern, go for any size or shape that pleases you. (Pumpkins can grow as large as 200 pounds!) If you are choosing pumpkins for cooking, ask the farmer for sugar pumpkins.

## STORING

Unlike their cousins, the winter squashes, pumpkins do not keep for long, usually for three to four weeks at room temperature and for six to eight weeks if refrigerated.

## PUTTING UP

Sugar pumpkins can be canned or frozen as puree. However, unless you are a purist,

*Sugar pumpkins*

canned pumpkin puree is so inexpensive and just as tasty as the real thing that making it yourself is not worth the effort. Pumpkins cannot be dried and will not keep in cold storage.

## PREPARING

Sugar pumpkins can be boiled, steamed, baked, or sautéed in the same manner as other winter squashes.

**PEPITAS.** If you love toasted pumpkin seeds and have a fair amount of patience, reserve the seeds that you scoop from your annual jack-o'-lantern. Allow them to air-dry overnight, then hull them. Toss the hulled seeds with a bit of vegetable oil, spread them on a baking sheet, and bake them in a 400°F oven for about 30 minutes. Salt to taste.

**JACK-O'-LANTERNS OR LUMINARIES.** Anybody can make a cute Halloween jack-o'-lantern. First, select a pumpkin.

Keeping the pumpkin's stem as the handle and using a very sharp chef's knife, cut a round "lid" from the top. Carefully scoop out the seeds and fibers, creating a smooth finish on the inside.

Using a felt-tip pen, draw a face on the side of the pumpkin. (Or, for a more sophisticated design, draw stars, circles, or crescents.) Again using the chef's knife, cut out the face or the designs. (Or try using a battery-operated or electric screwdriver to make the holes.) Insert a votive candle inside and replace the lid.

## SERVING SUGGESTIONS

Sugar pumpkins can be used in precisely the same manner as other winter squashes, including as a mashed side dish, or they can be made into a puree for soups and baked goods, such as cakes, cookies, muffins, and, of course, pies.

# QUINCE

The quince has been a delicacy in many cuisines of the world, especially Greek, Turkish, and Middle Eastern, for thousands of years. Most people have at least heard of quince jelly, yet somehow quince is still considered too exotic for most Americans, at least in its fresh form. Still, a few regional farmers cultivate a few quince trees, and the fruit is occasionally available at Greenmarket.

A quince looks rather like a large, lumpy Golden Delicious apple, although with a slightly darker green coloring and cream-colored flesh that is much denser and dryer than an apple's. The flavor is rather apple-like (although some people compare quinces to pears), although quinces are tarter than apples.

## SELECTING

Select large fruits that are firm and more yellow than green. On average, although quinces are larger, have thicker skin, and

can be lumpier than a Golden Delicious apple, choose one that is about the same size.

## STORING

Place quinces in a plastic bag and store in the vegetable crisper of the refrigerator; they will last for two to three weeks.

## PUTTING UP

Quinces have lots of natural pectin, and therefore make up into jelly quite easily. They can also be made into butter in the same way that you make apple butter. Quinces cannot be frozen or dried.

## PREPARING

Because the skin of a quince is thicker and tarter than an apple's or pear's, peel quinces before cooking or serving raw.

## SERVING SUGGESTIONS

Quinces are not usually consumed out of hand or raw; they tend to be too tart or thick to suit the American palate. Like apples and pears, they make delicious jams, jellies, butters, and other preserves. They can also be baked solo or in pies or tarts. Or they can be stewed, fried, or baked as a savory side dish with meat.

*Poe Park Greenmarket, The Bronx*

---

### BAKED QUINCES WITH HONEY
#### Serves 4

*Serve as an interesting dessert, particularly after a spicy or savory meal.*

> 3 large quinces
> 1 teaspoon ground cinnamon
> 1 cup honey
> Sour cream or heavy cream

Preheat the oven to 300°F. Peel the quinces, core, and cut into slices about ¼-inch thick. Arrange slices in a heavy casserole. Sprinkle with cinnamon, pour the honey over the slices, and add enough water to cover. Bake for about 1 hour, or until the fruit is tender. Cool and serve with sour cream or heavy cream.

---

# RADISHES

When we think of radishes, we usually conjure up marble-shaped red vegetables (classic red Globes) with snowy white flesh. The fact is, radishes come in many varieties. Radishes are root vegetables that are closely related to the cabbage family. Their leaves are edible and resemble kale in some varieties. Like their cousins, radishes are high in vitamin C, low in calories, and very flavorful.

## VARIETIES

There are many varieties of radish. Among those available at Greenmarket are:

**BLACK RADISH.** A native of northern and eastern Europe, the black radish

(which, itself, comes in several varieties, including the Black Spanish) is black only on the outside; its flesh is pure white. It is crisp and dry in texture with a very pungent, peppery flavor. Black radishes are best eaten judiciously—sliced, grated, or shredded on other foods.

**DAIKON RADISH.** The Daikon radish is a native of Japan and is well known as a

garnish or grated in miso soup. Daikons are long and cylindrical, cream-colored on the outside and white on the inside. They are larger than other radishes, and can grow as large as 2 pounds.

**FLAMBOYANT RADISH.** This oblong radish is red with a white top. Flamboyant radishes arrive in early summer and are available throughout the warmer months. They taste like Globes.

**GLOBE RADISH.** Globe radishes are round, about 1 inch in diameter, and are especially delicious in early spring, when they are tiny. They can grow to as much as 2 inches in diameter, but become pithy if they get too big. They are usually a beautiful bluish red but can be purple or white.

**ROSE FLESH RADISH (OR CHINA ROSE).** The Rose Flesh radish is a native of China, and has been cultivated in the United States for its lush yet delicate beauty. Pearly white on the outside, its flesh is jewel-pink. The flavor of the radish is spicy, sweet, and particularly delicious. The Chinese use Rose Flesh radishes to create the exquisite butterflies, birds, swans, and flowers that decorate banquet platters. You can also simply slice them thinly into salads or serve them as part of a crudité platter.

**TAEBAEK RADISH.** A native of Korea, the Taebaek radish looks much like the Rose Flesh radish on the outside, with a pale, creamy green coloring, but its flesh is pure white. It has a very strong and peppery flavor. It is an ideal radish for pickling or using as a thinly sliced garnish on salads.

## SELECTING

From spring throughout summer, radishes come tied in bunches, with their leaves attached. By late fall, the greens will have faded and only the roots are available. The roots of many radish varieties remain delicious throughout the winter.

## STORING

Trim the leaves before storing, leaving about 1 inch of stem on the radishes. Store the roots, unwashed, in the vegetable crisper of the refrigerator.

## PUTTING UP

The only way to preserve radishes is by storing them in a root cellar—which is why they are available at Greenmarket throughout the winter. (The exception is Red Globe radishes, which cannot be preserved and should be consumed within seven days of harvest.) Radishes cannot be canned, frozen, or dried.

## PREPARING

Trim the greens. (Use the leafy greens in salads or to flavor soups and stews.)

*Globe radishes*

Using a vegetable brush, gently scrub the radishes. Grate or slice the radishes with a stainless-steel (noncarbon steel) chef's knife, a good grater, or in a food processor fitted with a grating blade.

## SERVING SUGGESTIONS

Young, milder radishes, especially Red Globes, can be served whole and raw as part of a crudité platter. (Their peppery flavor combines well with coarse salt.) Or they can be sautéed and served as a side dish. If you are deft with a sharp knife, create radish "roses" or other decorative pieces with Red Globe, China Rose, Daikon, or even black radishes.

Sharp-flavored, mature radishes can be grated and used as flavoring in canapés, soups, stews, casseroles, salads, and slaws.

*French icicle radishes*

## PUMPERNICKEL BREAD WITH GRATED BLACK & ROSE RADISHES
### Makes 24 canapés

*This is a simple, rustic canapé—and a very flavorful one as well. The white and pink flesh from the radishes makes a pretty confetti-like mélange.*

- 1 black radish
- 1 Rose Flesh (China Rose) radish
- 5 thin slices pumpernickel bread
- 1 stick (½ cup) unsalted butter, softened

  Coarse salt

Grate the radishes. In a medium-sized bowl, toss the grated radishes together. (If you prefer, you can keep the radish flesh separate and serve two different types of canapé.) Quarter the bread slices.

Spread each bread quarter with butter and mound a generous portion of the grated radish on top. Sprinkle lightly with coarse salt. Serve immediately.

○ ● ● ●
W  S  S  F

# John Gorzynski

### Gorzynski Organic Farm • Sullivan County
### Cochecton Center, New York 12727
Union Square (Manhattan)

John Gorzynski has been a stone in the bedrock of Greenmarket since 1979. Although he grows a range of vegetables, John's specialty is root vegetables, from potatoes and parsnips to the exotic Rose Flesh radish. He also has a special interest in wild edibles like horseradish, burdock, salsify, chickweed, and purslane, which he both cultivates and harvests from natural growth.

John, who studied forestry at the University of New Hampshire, learned much about farming from his parents (who did not own a farm, but were avid home gardeners) and his grandfather (who grew up on a farm that was located in the Bronx near the present Bronx-Whitestone Bridge, and later owned another farm in Oradell, New Jersey). John always knew he wanted to become a farmer, and began learning his trade by working some land owned by his parents in northern New Jersey. In 1992, he bought his own 52-acre farm (only 20 acres of which are cultivated) in Cochecthen Center, Sullivan County, deep in the Catskill mountains.

When John began selling at Greenmarket, he worked at the now-defunct Gansevoort Greenmarket, which was close to where his grandfather had sold produce two generations ago. In more recent years, John has been a fixture at the Union Square market.

With his quiet but friendly manner, John is a pleasure to talk to. Stop by his stand as you stroll through the market. You may be shocked to find yourself falling in love with a radish.

# RAMPS

Ramp, which is native to eastern North America, is a wild plant, a relative of the onion and leek, and resembles a scallion, although its leaves are rounder and smoother. Its flavor is onion/garlic-like, at once savory yet sweet. Ramps are in season in the spring and are available from mid-April until early June.

## SELECTING

Look for bright green, smooth leaves without signs of wilting or brown spots. Roots should appear fresh, crisp, and white. Very young ramps have a pinkish hue, may be limp, and are very sweet.

## STORING

Store ramps, unwashed, in a plastic bag in the vegetable crisper of the refrigerator. They will keep for three to four days.

## PUTTING UP

Ramps cannot be canned or dried. They can be frozen—chopped—in an airtight container or a plastic freezer bag, and will keep in the freezer for a year.

*Verdi Square Greenmarket, Manhattan*

Photo © Tony Manetta

## PREPARING

Trim any brown off the leaves and the "beard" off the white root. Pull off any moist layers on the roots. Ramps can be steamed, braised, or sautéed.

## SERVING SUGGESTIONS

Ramps can be substituted for leeks, scallions, or onions in virtually any recipe. They can be served as a side dish, or added to soups, salads, sauces, dressings, casseroles, and stir-fries.

## RAMP VICHYSSOISE
### Serves 4

*Ramps are sometimes called "wild leeks,"
so incorporating them into a traditional
Vichyssoise recipe seems appropriate. Despite its
French name, vichyssoise was created by chef
Louis Diat in 1910 at the old Ritz-Carlton
Hotel that stood on Madison Avenue.*

|   |   |
|---|---|
| 2 | tablespoons butter |
| 12 to 18 | ramps, washed, trimmed, and chopped |
| 2 | leeks, washed, trimmed, and cut crosswise into rounds |
| 1 | white onion, coarsely chopped |
| 6 | medium-sized white potatoes, peeled and thinly sliced |
| 3 | cups chicken broth or water |
| 1 | teaspoon ground nutmeg |
|   | Salt |
| 2 | cups whole milk |
| ¼ | teaspoon white pepper |
| 1 | cup heavy cream |
|   | Chopped fresh ramps, roots and leaves, for garnish |

Melt the butter in a large, heavy saucepan over medium heat. Add the ramps, leeks, and onion and cook until translucent and limp, but not brown, about 8 minutes. Add the potatoes, chicken broth, nutmeg, and 1 tablespoon of salt, and bring to a boil; reduce the heat and simmer until the potatoes are very soft, about 30 minutes.

Transfer the vegetables to the bowl of a blender and puree until very smooth. Return the puree to the saucepan, add the milk, and heat through, but do not allow the soup to boil. Add the white pepper and season with salt to taste. Swirl in the heavy cream, but do not cook further. Chill the soup. Serve cold, garnished with chopped fresh ramps.

*Scallions are look-alike cousins to ramps*

# RHUBARB

Botanically, rhubarb is related to celery, which is not surprising since it looks like rose-colored celery. However, most people use it the way they would a tartly flavored fruit: stewed (slightly sweetened with sugar or honey), as a dessert sauce, or in pies. (In some regions of the country, rhubarb is called pie plant.) Rhubarb arrives at Greenmarket in May and lasts until mid-June.

## SELECTING

Choose large, well-colored, straight, firm stalks. Leaves should be fresh and crisp; smaller leaves indicate more tender stalks. It is important to note that rhubarb leaves are poisonous and should never be eaten.

## STORING

Because the rhubarb leaves are toxic, remove the leaves as soon as you get home and before you store them. Place the stalks in a plastic bag and store in the refrigerator. Rhubarb keeps for one week.

## Putting Up

Rhubarb freezes well if it will be used for making jams, sauces, or stews. To freeze, cut the ribs into chunks, blanch them quickly to preserve the color, place them in an airtight freezer container, and freeze. Rhubarb can also be frozen as syrup or puree.

Rhubarb can be canned, but freezing is easier and results in better color, flavor, and texture. It can be made into jelly, jam, or chutney. Rhubarb cannot be dried.

## Preparing

Trim the leaves, wash thoroughly, then cut off rough ends and remove any coarse fibers with a paring knife. Rhubarb can be baked or stewed. To bake it, cut the stalks into 1-inch pieces, place in a glass baking dish, sprinkle with sugar—about ½ cup per pound—and bake for about 30 minutes in a 300°F oven.

## Serving Suggestions

Rhubarb is wonderful baked in pies, quick breads, and muffins. Stewed rhubarb is tasty on its own, but, given its tart flavor, it helps to stew it with a sweet fruit. Strawberries are a perennial favorite, but also try pineapple, apples, pears, or raspberries, or else sweeten it with maple syrup, honey, or orange juice. Stewed rhubarb sauce is delicious over pound cake, angel food cake, ice cream, and yogurt, or served with whipped cream.

Rhubarb can also be used to make a savory sauce to serve with duck or chicken.

---

### SIMPLE STEWED RHUBARB
**Serves 4**

*Add 1 cup of sliced strawberries to the ingredients for a classic combination.*

> 1 pound rhubarb stalks
> ¼ cup sugar
> 1 teaspoon coarsely grated lemon zest
> ¼ cup orange juice

Wash and trim the rhubarb stalks and cut into 1-inch chunks. Place the rhubarb in a heavy saucepan. Add the sugar, grated lemon zest, and orange juice; cover; and cook gently over low to medium heat for about 15 minutes. Serve warm with whipped cream or over ice cream.

---

# SCALLIONS

Scallions are immature—or "baby"—onions. Often referred to as green onions, they are harvested while the tops are still green and the bulb has not developed. They have a milder, sweeter flavor than onions and can be substituted for them in almost any recipe. In our region, because of multiple plantings, scallions are available at the market from early spring throughout autumn.

## SELECTING

Look for bright green, crisp leaves without any signs of wilting or brown spots. Check the white ends, which should appear pure white, fresh, and firm.

## STORING

Unlike mature onions, scallions are quite perishable and cannot be stored at room temperature or in cold storage. Instead, store scallions, unwashed, in a plastic bag in the vegetable crisper of the refrigerator. They will keep for three to four days.

## PUTTING UP

Scallions cannot be dried or canned. They can be chopped and frozen in an airtight container or plastic freezer bag. They will keep in the freezer for about a year.

## PREPARING

Trim off the "beard" from the white root, and trim off any wilted parts from the greens. Depending upon the recipe, both the green and the white parts of the scallion can be used. Sometimes the outer skin becomes vaguely slimy and should be peeled off before preparing.

## SERVING SUGGESTIONS

Since scallions are simply young onions, they can be substituted for onions in virtually any recipe, although their flavor is less strong. They can also be substituted for chives, although their flavor is usually stronger.

Scallions are a common ingredient in Chinese and other Asian cuisines, often used instead of onions. Because they are milder than onions and cook a bit faster, they can be added easily to stir-fries. In Asian cuisines, scallions are often cut creatively and used as a decorative garnish.

Scallions can also be used as a flavoring in rice dishes, pasta sauces, casseroles, and any dish where a mild oniony flavor is desired.

## CHAMP
### Serves 6

*Champ, like Colcannon, is Irish comfort food. Instead of cabbage as a flavoring, champ features scallions. You can substitute parsley or nettles for the chives.*

- 1½ cups milk
- 10 scallions, chopped
- 3 tablespoons chives, chopped
- 6 cups hot mashed potatoes (5 to 6 potatoes boiled and mashed)
- Salt and freshly ground pepper
- 4 tablespoons butter, melted

Bring the milk to a boil in a large nonreactive saucepan. Add the scallions and the chives and boil until crisp/tender. Drain and reserve the milk. Add the scallions and chives to the mashed potatoes and beat, adding enough of the hot milk to make the dish creamy. Season to taste with salt and pepper. Pile into a deep serving bowl, make a well in the middle of the potatoes, and pour in the butter.

# SPINACH

Spinach is a familiar presence in many Mediterranean cuisines, but for some reason it has gotten a bad reputation among American children. True, spinach is a rather strong-tasting green; its flavor is more pronounced than most lettuces. But its leaves are tender (which is not true of some other greens) and it works deliciously as a side dish, either cooked or raw.

## SELECTING

Look for dark green, crisp leaves. Avoid leaves that are yellowing, moldy-looking, or too wet.

## STORING

Store spinach, unwashed, in a perforated plastic bag, in the vegetable crisper of the refrigerator. Spinach will stay fresh for about three days.

## PUTTING UP

Spinach cannot be dried or canned, but it freezes easily, either chopped or as a puree or for use later in cooked dishes.

## PREPARING

Because spinach grows in sandy soil, it comes to market filled with grit. To avoid the tell-tale crunch, three or four washings are required. (Ancient cookbooks talk about washing it a minimum of 12 times, the last time using tears instead of water.)

To wash, remove any damaged leaves and tough stems. Give the leaves a quick shower under the tap, then place them in a sink or deep pan filled with cool water. Allow the spinach to soak for ten minutes and the silt to sink to the bottom. Change the water and soak it again—and again— until the silt is gone.

Use a stainless-steel knife for chopping spinach; a carbon-steel knife will leave black marks on the leaves, and the spinach will discolor the knife's blade. Avoid cooking spinach in aluminum or cast-iron pans or serving it in silver dishes.

Steam spinach in a heavy nonreactive saucepan. Don't add water; the spinach will require only the water that is on the leaves to steam. Cover tightly and cook the spinach over low heat for about five minutes per pound, or until the spinach wilts.

Spinach that is to be used as salad greens should be thoroughly dried.

## SERVING SUGGESTIONS

Spinach is a delicious addition to a multi-green salad, and can carry a salad on its own. Spinach is a flavorful side dish with just about any meat, chicken, or fish. It combines so well with eggs and cheese that it is often used in savory tarts, risottos, and other egg or cheese dishes, and is used to make green pastas.

### GROOVY SPINACH SALAD
#### Serves 2 as a main dish

*In the 1960s, Allen's Bar, on Manhattan's Upper East Side, served a great spinach salad. This is my memory of that dish.*

| | |
|---|---|
| 1 | pound fresh spinach |
| 2 | garlic cloves, minced |
| 2 | tablespoons olive oil |
| 4 | teaspoons balsamic vinegar |
| 1 | tablespoon whole-grain mustard |
| ½ | teaspoon ground nutmeg |
| | Salt and freshly ground black pepper |
| 4 | scallions, cleaned, trimmed, and coarsely chopped |
| 4 | ounces cooked bacon, crumbled |
| 2 | hard-cooked eggs, sliced |

Trim the stems and wash and dry the spinach thoroughly. Place the minced garlic in the bottom of a large salad bowl. Add the olive oil, vinegar, mustard, nutmeg, and salt and pepper to taste; whisk the dressing until it is smooth. Add the chopped scallions and toss. Add the spinach leaves and toss to combine. Sprinkle the bacon over the salad and top with the egg slices. Serve immediately.

# SPRING BLOSSOMS

*Cherry blossoms*

Spring is one of the most exciting times at Greenmarket. The thrill is enhanced by the early arrival of spring blossoms, especially those from apple, cherry, and peach trees. These blossoms are not idly foraged by the growers. They must come from the growers' own property, or from property that is rented or leased by the grower within 20 miles of his home farm.

## VARIETIES

### APPLE, PEACH, AND OTHER BLOSSOMS.
Branches of apple, peach, cherry, and plum trees that produce beautiful and fragrant blossoms before they produce fruit. Fruit tree blossoms are readily available at Greenmarket beginning in mid-April.

### DOGWOOD.
A small, decorative tree whose branches produce large, fleshy pink or white blossoms.

### FORSYTHIA.
A shrub that produces long, whip-like stems with tiny leaves and a profusion of yellow flowers.

### LILACS.
A fragrant shrub that is available in abundance for about a month beginning in late April. The flowers are usually lavender, but they can be rose, pink, or white.

**PUSSY WILLOW.** A shrub that produces long, leggy stems and tiny gray fuzzy buds. They bloom at the same time as forsythia, and make a pretty bouquet on their own or as filler with other blossoms or spring cut flowers.

## SELECTING

Choose heavily budded steams or branches. If blossoms have appeared, look for fresh, perky, fragrant flowers and bright green, fresh leaves.

## PREPARING

To prepare the stems to accept water easily, scrape the bark away for about 2 inches from the bottom of the stem, then split the end up about 2 inches. (If the stem is particularly thick and woody, you may need to smash it with a hammer.) Immerse the base of the stems in boiling water for about 30 seconds, then plunge them into cool water. They will flower in about 24 hours. Blossoms should last for five to seven days, depending upon the variety of bloom and how close it was to flowering.

## FORCING BLOOMS.

Encouraging tree and shrub blossoms to bloom a few weeks before their natural time is referred to as forcing. In our region, blossoms can be forced from mid- to late March, and usually forceable stems begin to show up at the market at this time.

To force blooms, remove all the twigs and leaves from the stems. Peel back the bark, split the end of the branch or stem up about 2 inches, and submerge the stems in warm water. The buds will appear within 24 to 48 hours, and the stems will blossom shortly thereafter.

## DISPLAYING

Arrange long stems, particularly softer, more whip-like stems like forsythia, in a tall, narrow vase that will hold them upright. Combine different varieties of flowering stems, especially the various fruit boughs or forsythia, with pussy willow, to create a traditional spring arrangement.

Another way to show off spring blossoms is to cut the longer stemmed varieties (especially pussy willow and forsythia) down to about 12 to 15 inches in height and combine them with cut spring flowers, such as daffodils and tulips.

# SPROUTS & SHOOTS

Any bean or seed can be sprouted, and sometimes the young shoot of a plant is as delicious as the mature vegetable. Many sprouts are grown indoors, hydroponically, and several growers offer a variety of them year-round.

## VARIETIES

Many varieties of sprouts and shoots are available at Greenmarket, including:

**ALFALFA SPROUTS.** Thread-like sprouts with tiny seed-like tops.

**BEANS SPROUTS.** Larger and more succulent than alfalfa sprouts, these sprouts (from mung beans) are also more watery.

**BROCCOLI SHOOTS.** The shoots of broccoli seeds; available in several varieties.

**BUCKWHEAT SPROUTS.** Young shoots of buckwheat; they look and taste like clover.

**LENTIL SPROUTS.** Silky threads with seeds, these have a smooth texture.

**RADISH SPROUTS.** Daikon radish sprouts are well known; they have a silky texture and tangy flavor.

**SNOW PEA SHOOTS.** Tender shoots of the snow pea plant, they resemble young spinach in taste, but are more delicate. (See recipe, opposite.)

**SOYBEAN SPROUTS.** Look like mung bean sprouts and have a similar texture but a stronger flavor.

**SUNFLOWER SPROUTS.** Similar in flavor to alfalfa sprouts but a bit more succulent and crunchier in texture.

*Broccoli shoots*

*Buckwheat sprouts*

*Radish sprouts*

*Sunflower sprouts*

## SELECTING

Choose crisp, moist sprouts that look and smell fresh and clean. Avoid sprouts that are discolored or appear slimy or moldy.

## STORING

Store sprouts and shoots, unwashed and loosely packed, in a plastic bag in the refrigerator. They will keep for two to three days.

## PUTTING UP

Sprouts and shoots cannot be canned, frozen, preserved, or dried. Like other delicate greens, they must be eaten fresh.

## PREPARING

Wash the sprouts and shoots gently under cool water. If they have begun to wilt, soak them in ice water for about ten minutes.

## SERVING SUGGESTIONS

Sprouts and shoots can be an alternative to lettuce in salads and sandwiches. (Avocado and sprouts in pita bread is a vegetarian classic.) Sprouts also add flavor and texture to omelettes, frittatas, and other cooked dishes. They are delicious as part of a stir-fry, but should not be added until the last few seconds of cooking.

---

### GRACE YOUNG'S STIR-FRIED SNOW PEA SHOOTS
**Serves 4 as part of a multicourse meal**

*This recipe comes from Grace Young's wonderful cookbook* Wisdom of the Chinese Kitchen.

- 8 ounces snow pea shoots (about 16 cups loosely packed)
- 2 tablespoons vegetable oil
- 1 clove garlic, crushed and peeled
- ¼ teaspoon salt

Wash shoots in several changes of cold water and drain thoroughly in a colander until dry to the touch.

Heat a 14-inch flat-bottomed wok or heavy skillet over high heat until hot but not smoking. Add 1 tablespoon vegetable oil and garlic, and stir-fry about 1 minute. Add the remaining tablespoon vegetable oil, salt, and snow pea shoots, and stir-fry, shaking wok occasionally, 2 to 3 minutes, or until leaves begin to soften. Continue stir-frying until the vegetables are just tender but bright green, about 1 minute. Serve immediately.

---

# STRAWBERRIES

The appearance of strawberries at Greenmarket is one of the first signs that summer has arrived. For three or four weeks, like corn and tomatoes a short time later, strawberries dominate the scene. Then, like all things exquisite, delicate, and much-loved, they are gone.

## VARIETIES

**TRI-STARS.** In addition to the regular variety strawberry, in recent years several farmers have cultivated Tri-Stars, which are available in September and October. Tri-Stars, which were developed in this region, ripen without needing as much sunshine as early summer varieties. The berries tend to be small and very sweet.

## SELECTING

Look for bright red, plump, shiny, well-formed berries with no sign of mold or wetness. The caps should be fresh, crisp, and green.

## STORING

Remove strawberries from the container, if the farmer has not done so already. Discard any bruised or soggy fruit and place the remainder in a colander, bowl, or spread out on a plate lined with paper towels and cover with plastic wrap. Store them, unwashed, in the refrigerator. Strawberries will last two days at the most.

## PUTTING UP

Like other berries, strawberries can be frozen. Wash the berries, hull them, then lay them on a baking sheet and freeze them until hard. Transfer them to a freezer bag.

## PREPARING

Sort the berries and discard any that have become too soft or have mold. Just before using, wash the berries quickly and carefully under cold water, drain, and pat dry. Hull the berries, or, if you are serving large, succulent berries whole, leave the caps on.

## SERVING SUGGESTIONS

Serve strawberries whole (with their caps on) or sliced, plain or sprinkled with sugar. They are also delicious with heavy cream, whipped cream, ice cream, crème fraîche, yogurt, or sherbet. Like melon, strawberries can be served at any meal: For breakfast, they can be sprinkled on cereal, waffles, or pancakes, or cooked in muffins or other quick breads. Strawberries also combine well with other fruits and berries and are a must in a fruit compote or salad or as part of a fruit smoothie. Strawberries are delicious in pies, tarts, crêpes, shortcake, puddings, mousses, and soufflés.

## STRAWBERRIES WITH BALSAMIC VINEGAR & BLACK PEPPER
### Serves 4

*This recipe is from Mario Batali's wonderful book* Simple Italian Food: Recipes from My Two Villages. *It is very old-fashioned, very Italian, and very delicious.*

> 2  pints strawberries, hulled,
>    if large, cut in half
> 2  tablespoons best-quality balsamic
>    vinegar
> 1  teaspoon sugar
>    Freshly ground black pepper

In a medium mixing bowl, toss the strawberries, vinegar, and sugar together well. Divide among 4 martini glasses or other pretty glass dishes. Drizzle all the vinegar over the fruit. Grind fresh black pepper over each portion and serve.

# Sweet Potatoes

Sweet potatoes are often confused with yams. To make this sweet potato/yam issue even more complicated, sweet potatoes come in several varieties, ranging from a pale yellow variety to a bright orange variety. The yellow variety has a thin skin, pale yellow flesh, and a denser texture. The brighter variety has a thicker, dark orange skin and bright orange flesh that is moister and sweeter than the pale variety. True yams are cultivated in Africa, the Caribbean, and the American South.

## Selecting

Like many root vegetables, sweet potatoes can grow quite large. Choose small- to medium-sized potatoes with skin as smooth as you can find. Avoid potatoes with spots or extended roots. Sweet potatoes are available from late September through the winter.

## Storing

Store sweet potatoes, unwashed, in a cool, dry place. Do not refrigerate. Sweet potatoes are more perishable than ordinary potatoes. They will keep for four weeks.

## Putting Up

Sweet potatoes can be canned (using the hot-pack method), frozen (whole, sliced, or pureed), and dried (use the yellow ones combined with white potatoes).

## PREPARING

The pale variety of sweet potato can be prepared in precisely the same way as white potatoes (see page 197). Before cooking, scrub gently, remove any blemishes, and proceed. The orange variety is sweeter and mushier. Boil both types of sweet potatoes before peeling; the skins slip easily off the cooked potatoes.

## SERVING SUGGESTIONS

Serve the pale variety as you would serve white potatoes: boiled, roasted, mashed, or fried. For an interesting change of pace, make a mélange of potatoes, both white and sweet.

Serve the orange variety as an alternative to white potatoes or winter squash. The orange variety, especially when served mashed or whipped, combines well with brown sugar, maple syrup, as well as the sweeter spices such as cinnamon, ginger, and nutmeg. The orange variety makes interesting French fried potatoes, especially when seasoned with herbs and spices instead of just salt.

## RACHEL'S LOW-CALORIE ROASTED SWEET POTATO CHIPS
### Serves 4

*My friend Rachel Ginsburg, who is a terrific skier, manages to maintain an equally terrific figure without appearing to deny herself too many treats. Every afternoon, after a day on the slopes, Rachel fixes these sweet potato chips. The happy fact is that these chips are both nutritious and not particularly fattening.*

> 3 to 4  medium-sized sweet potatoes
> Nonstick vegetable spray
> Salt

Preheat the oven to 400°F. Scrub the potatoes under cool water. Peel or scrape the skin (or leave it on—which is more nutritious—as you prefer), and slice the potatoes as thinly as possible. Spray a baking sheet with vegetable spray, arrange the sliced potatoes evenly on the sheet, and spray lightly with the vegetable spray. Salt to taste. Bake the chips, uncovered, until the chips begin to curl and turn a golden brown, about 15 minutes. Serve hot.

# TOMATILLOS & HUSK CHERRIES

Tomatillos look like pale green or pearly yellow cherry tomatoes, while husk cherries look like green grapes. Both come in a delicate papery pod, or "husk" (called a calyx), that must be removed before eating. Both also have a fruity flavor; tomatillos have a grapefruit-lemon flavor and husk cherries have an apple-grape taste.

### SELECTING
In both cases, select specimens with clean, dry husks and firm, smooth fruit.

### STORING
Store them, in their husks, in a paper bag in the refrigerator. They will last as long as two weeks.

### PUTTING UP
Tomatillos and husk cherries are best preserved as part of a relish. Freezing and drying are not effective.

### PREPARING
Remove the husks, stem, and wash the little tomatoes. For dishes using these vegetables,

*Husk cherries*

Tomatillos, which means "little tomatoes" in Spanish (they are also known as Mexican green tomatoes and jamberries), have become a very popular item at Greenmarket. Their little cousins, the husk cherries (also called husk tomatoes, ground cherries, or cape gooseberries), are almost as celebrated.

whether cooked or raw, you probably will not need to remove the skin, which, in fact, contributes much to their texture and flavor.

## SERVING SUGGESTIONS

Substitute tomatillos and husk cherries for just about any recipe in which you would be using cherry tomatoes, although the flavor will be more fruity.

Tomatillos are perfect for salsa crudas (served with chips or raw vegetables), as part of a salad, or cooked into a salsa verde to serve with poultry, fish, enchiladas, or other Mexican dishes. They can also be grilled, broiled, or baked.

*Tomatillos*

### GREENMARKET SALSA CRUDA
#### Makes 3 cups

*Serve with tortilla chips, crudités, shrimp— or even chicken fingers.*

| | |
|---|---|
| 1 | pound fresh tomatillos |
| ½ | pound cherry tomatoes |
| 2 | chipotle chilies, minced |
| 1 | jalapeño chili, minced |
| 2 | medium onions, minced |
| 4 | garlic cloves, minced |
| 1 | tablespoon fresh lime juice |
| 1 | tablespoon balsamic vinegar |
| 2 | tablespoons fresh cilantro, finely chopped |

Peel papery husks from the tomatillos and husk tomatoes, and rinse. Chop the tomatillos and tomatoes coarsely. In a nonreactive bowl, combine them with all the remaining ingredients and chill before serving.

Tiny husk cherries can be served raw, as a snack (they are zesty and low in calories). When halved or chopped, they are a nice addition to salads and salsas, and can also be cooked as a savory side relish to serve with meats and savory pies.

# Tomatoes

Nothing hails the arrival of summer more dramatically than fire-engine red tomatoes. And no gourmet-store tomato can compare to the delicious flavor of a homegrown variety.

## Varieties

**Beefsteak tomatoes** are large, bright red, and so succulent that they tend to flatten out or become elliptical. They are best eaten raw in salads or sliced on sandwiches.

**Globe tomatoes** are medium- to large-sized (the larger the more flavorful) round tomatoes that can be green, red, or yellow. (Yellow globes are sweeter than red.) Select globes for salads, sandwiches, and juices.

**Green tomatoes** are simply unripened tomatoes. They are less sweet, but are delicious fried or preserved. Green tomatoes will continue to ripen after picking, but will never be as sweet and flavorful as vine-riped tomatoes.

**Plum (or Italian) tomatoes** are small, egg-shaped tomatoes. They seem pulpier and sweeter than globe tomatoes, and are perfect for sauces, soups, and stewed tomatoes, other side dishes.

**Cherry tomatoes** are like miniature globe tomatoes; they come in red, yellow, orange, and green varieties, and can be used for hors d'oeuvres, salads, and kabobs.

**Pear tomatoes** are small, red or yellow pear-shaped tomatoes. They are very sweet and can be used instead of cherry tomatoes.

**Currant (or Grape) tomatoes** are the size of a grape, come in red and yellow varieties, and are sweet and crispy.

**Heirloom tomatoes** are old-fashioned tomato varieties, and in recent years, many Greenmarket growers have been experimenting with them. They vary in size from as small as a grape (Green Grape) to as large as a softball, and come in a spectrum of colors, from red, orange, yellow, and green to purple and even brown.

*Globe tomatoes at various stages of ripeness*

## SELECTING

Choose tomatoes that are firm, well shaped, richly colored for their variety, fragrant, heavy for their size, and somewhat soft (but not too soft). Avoid tomatoes with too many scars or blemishes. Remember, however, organically grown tomatoes, especially heirlooms, will naturally have a few marks which will not affect flavor and can be easily removed.

*Cherry tomatoes*     *Plum tomatoes*

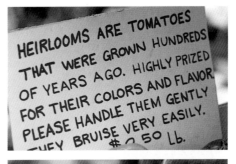

HEIRLOOMS ARE TOMATOES
THAT WERE GROWN HUNDREDS
OF YEARS AGO. HIGHLY PRIZED
FOR THEIR COLORS AND FLAVOR.
PLEASE HANDLE THEM GENTLY
THEY BRUISE VERY EASILY.
$2.50 Lb.

*Currant tomatoes with chili pepper to show scale*

*Heirloom tomatoes*

## STORING

Store ripe tomatoes at room temperature; refrigeration makes the skin flabby and the texture mealy. Avoid storing tomatoes in direct sunlight, which can ripen them unevenly. Instead, place them on a shelf, stem-side down. To ripen them faster, store them in a brown paper bag with an apple. Use ripe tomatoes within two or three days.

## PUTTING UP

Tomatoes can be frozen whole or chopped, for use later in cooked dishes, or they can be made into a sauce and frozen. Tomatoes can be canned whole or as a sauce, soup, or juice. Tomatoes can be preserved as ketchup, piccalilli, marmalade, chili sauce, and all sorts of other preserves. They sun-dry beautifully, but the process requires special equipment and conditions.

## PREPARING

The skin can be left on when tomatoes are served raw or baked (and the skin is needed to hold the tomato together). When tomatoes are to be cooked into sauces, the skins should be removed. To remove the skin, blanch the tomato in boiling water for 30 seconds, remove it with a slotted spoon, then slit the skin and pull it off with your fingers. (It will slide off easily.) Before adding peeled tomatoes to a sauce, coarsely chop them, press them through a strainer, reserving the juice and discarding the seeds.

## SERVING SUGGESTIONS

Tomatoes can be used raw or cooked in salads, soups, sauces, and casseroles. Still, the best way to eat tomatoes in high summer is to slice them, season them with a bit of salt and pepper (or perhaps basil and good olive oil), and serve.

○ ○ ○ ○
W  S  S  F

# PAM CLARKE

PROSPECT HILL ORCHARD • Ulster County • Milton, New York 12547
Stands at Union Square, Verdi Square, Soho Square, Washington Market Park, and
Bowling Green (Manhattan)

One of the most exciting trends in farming today is the number of young people who have committed themselves to working the land. Even more fascinating is the high number of women who are joining these ranks. Pam Clarke is one of this new breed of growers.

One would think that Pam came to farming naturally. After all, she grew up on Prospect Hill Orchard, which has been an important Hudson Valley farm for over 200 years. Pam is the seventh generation Clarke to work on this land.

But when Pam graduated from William and Mary College with a degree in anthropology, she had no intention of farming. She tried a few management jobs, then headed for an adventure in Puerto Rico. While there, she met Robert Torres, and when she returned to New York, Robert came with her. (Today, Robert manages a stand at La Marketta in Spanish Harlem.)

When Pam returned from Puerto Rico, her dad, Steven Clarke, suggested that she take over the Greenmarket aspect of his business. Pam quickly realized that she loved it.

Traditionally, the Clarkes at Prospect Hill Orchard have cultivated tree fruits, including apples, peaches, pears, cherries, nectarines, plums, and apricots. They also grow berries and some vegetables. But Pam's interests have grown beyond the orchards. In addition to managing the Greenmarket business for Prospect Hill Orchard, she has leased a few acres of land from her dad and is growing her own crops, and she looks forward to experimenting with some exotic crops like figs, pawpaws, and hardy kiwi. It is a creative time in the farming business, and Pam Clarke is on the cutting edge.

# TURNIPS & RUTABAGAS

*Rutabaga*

Turnips and rutabagas, together with parsnips, are among the ranks of the less popular vegetables. They are considered old-fashioned, too strong-flavored, and, what's more, they have funny names. Too bad, because they are very interesting root vegetables.

## VARIETIES

Turnips and rutabagas are often treated the same, but they are different species.

**TURNIPS.** Pearly white with tinges of purple, turnips are shaped like a child's top. Baby turnips are sweet and succulent, especially when braised with their greens.

**RUTABAGAS.** Rutabagas are larger than turnips, with a tough beige-and-purple outer skin and dry, yellow flesh.

## SELECTING

Look for small turnips with smooth, creamy skins and bright fresh greens. Avoid both turnips or rutabagas if they are too big or their skin appears shriveled.

## STORING

Rutabagas and turnips store best in a root cellar. However, both can be stored in a plastic bag in the refrigerator; they will keep for several weeks. Baby turnips will stay sweet for about five days.

## PUTTING UP

Rutabagas and turnips can be frozen cubed (in a freezer bag or airtight container) or pureed. They are not normally canned or dried.

## PREPARING & SERVING

Baby turnips need not be peeled; older turnips do. To make peeling easier, blanch the turnips for about a minute, then peel. Rutabagas usually must be peeled. Both turnips and rutabagas can be steamed, pureed, roasted, or served raw as a crudité, in a salad or slaw. Both combine well with other vegetables, especially root vegetables, in soups, stews, or side dishes.

W S S F

### DEBORAH MADISON'S
### BUTTERED TURNIPS
### & RUTABAGAS
**Serves 4 to 6**

*An elegant but simple recipe.*

1½ pounds turnips and/or rutabagas, peeled
Salt and freshly ground pepper
2 tablespoons butter or sunflower oil
1 tablespoon chopped fresh parsley
2 teaspoons chopped fresh tarragon or thyme
2 tablespoons snipped chives
1 garlic clove, peeled and minced
½ cup fresh bread crumbs browned in 1 tablespoon butter

Cut the turnips and rutabagas into ½-inch cubes. Cook them separately in boiling salted water until they are tender-firm, about 12 minutes for the turnips and 20 minutes for the rutabagas. Drain. Melt the butter in a skillet over medium heat. When foamy, add the vegetables and sauté, stirring frequently, until golden. Toss with the herbs and the garlic, and season to taste with salt and pepper. Transfer to a serving dish and scatter the crisped bread crumbs over the top. Serve warm.

# WATERMELON

Watermelon is a fascinating member of the melon family. It commonly has a shocking pink flesh, but it can also be bright orange or yellow. (Yellow flesh watermelon is one of the most popular items at Greenmarket.) Watermelon is watery and sweet. This is for good reason: Watermelon is about 8 percent sugar and 92 percent water. It ripens in our region during the dog days of summer and remains available until shortly after Labor Day.

## VARIETIES

There are more than 50 varieties of watermelon, divided into two categories:

**PICNIC** watermelons weigh from 10 to 50 pounds and come in several shapes, usually round to oval. As their name suggests, these big guys are meant to be eaten outdoors (and enjoyed for their succulence) at a picnic or barbecue.

**ICE BOX** watermelons are smaller (that is, they can fit, whole, into the refrigerator) and can be round or oval.

## SELECTING

Watermelons are tricky to select. Relative ripeness is evidenced entirely by the color and condition of the skin and the sweet fragrance. (Most watermelons sold at Greenmarket will be ready to eat.)

The skin of watermelon should range from deep green to gray, and can be solid  or streaked with white. The underside may be paler because it has been resting on the ground and not exposed to the sun. The skin should be sort of waxy. If a stem is attached, it should be dry and brown; if the stem is green, it means the melon was picked before it was ripe. The melon should smell sweet.

If cut watermelons are displayed, check that the flesh is firm, well colored, and shows dark seeds. Avoid if the seeds have begun to separate from the flesh, or if the flesh exhibits white streaks or large cracks.

## STORING

A whole, uncut, watermelon can be stored at room temperature for about five days. It will not ripen further, but it will become juicier and more succulent. To chill, store it, whole (if it fits) or cut up, in the refrigerator. A whole watermelon will stay fresh for about a week in the refrigerator; a cut watermelon should be wrapped in plastic wrap and will last for three days.

## PUTTING UP

Watermelon can be frozen by removing all seeds, cutting the flesh into balls or cubes, packing it in a plastic freezer bag or con-

tainer, and placing it in the freezer. Frozen watermelon will last for about six months. Watermelon rind can be pickled.

## PREPARING

Using a large, sharp chef's knife, cut the watermelon into slices or wedges just before eating. Or cut the watermelon in half, scoop out all the flesh, and use the rind as a serving bowl for fruit salad. (Those with an artistic bent can scallop the rim.) Fill it with the flesh, cut into cubes or balls, combine it with other types of melon balls or berries, and sprinkle it lightly with sugar.

If the watermelon is to be served in balls or cubes, remove all seeds. If slices or wedges are served at a casual party or picnic, the seeds can be left in the flesh.

## SERVING SUGGESTIONS

Watermelon is the ideal dessert after a summer barbecue, picnic, or cold supper. It can be served in wedges on a plate, or cut into balls or cubes and served in bowls garnished with fresh mint. Watermelon combines well with all of its melon relations and with berries in a fruit compote. Watermelon, if you don't mind picking out the seeds, is a wonderful addition to fruit smoothies.

# WINTER SQUASH

*Carnival squash*

Scores of varieties of winter squash are available at Greenmarket. They begin to appear in late summer, and remain—to our great delight—well into darkest January.

## VARIETIES

**ACORN.** One of the best-loved squashes, it is acorn-shaped, has ridged skin, is dark green in color with orange markings, and has vivid orange flesh. Occasionally, a yellowish or a white variety is available.

**BANANA.** A large, cylindrical (or banana-shaped) squash that is pale yellow in color with orange flesh.

**BUTTERNUT.** A bell-shaped, tan-colored squash, that weighs from 2 to 5 pounds, and has bright orange, sweet flesh. Butternut is also one of the most nutritious squashes, being especially high in beta carotene and vitamin C.

**CARNIVAL.** A dark green and white speckled squash with orange flesh. Its flesh is somewhat stringy and dry.

**DELICATA.** An elongated squash, Delicata is white with green striations or

*Acorn squash*

*Hubbard squash*

*Butternut squash*

*Delicata squash*

yellow with orange striations. Its yellow flesh is sweet.

**GOLDEN NUGGET.** These little squashes look like baby pumpkins. They are delicious baked.

**HUBBARD.** Hubbards are big squashes that come in many varieties and colors, from dark green to bluish green to orange. They are not as sweet as Butternut or Delicata squashes.

**PUMPKIN.** Technically a winter squash, but with an allure all their own. (See Pumpkins, page 204.)

**SPAGHETTI.** An oval-shaped, pale yellow squash. When it is cooked, its flesh forms spaghetti-like strands.

**SWEET DUMPLING.** Sweet Dumplings look rather like little Delicata, and come in a variety of colors, from pale yellow to white with green striations.

**TURBAN.** Turbans resemble the Butternut in shape, but are usually larger and primarily orange with green striations.

## SELECTING

Unlike some vegetables, including summer squashes and eggplant, winter squashes become sweeter the longer they are allowed to grow. Look for smooth, dry rind, free of cracks, bruises, or spots. The rind should not be shiny; a shiny rind indicates immaturity and therefore lack of sweetness. The color should be bright and uniform, and the squash should feel heavy for its size. Look for squashes with the stem still attached; the stem should be dry.

Occasionally, cut squashes are for sale at Greenmarket. (Certain squashes, such as cheese squash, are too large for the average consumer, and therefore are sold in pieces.) When the flesh is visible, look for flesh that is bright, colorful, and finely grained.

## STORING

Store uncut squash in a cool, dry place; winter squash keeps for at least three months in cold storage. Don't store uncut squash in the refrigerator; the wetness will cause the squash to deteriorate. Store cut squash in the refrigerator, wrapped in plastic; it will keep for about two weeks.

*Various winter squash*

## PUTTING UP

Winter squash cans or freezes well, especially if pureed. Do not sweeten the squash before canning or freezing because it will alter the flavor, possibly making it bitter. It will keep for a year. Winter squash cannot be dried.

## PREPARING

Rinse off any dirt. To cut up the squash, use a heavy chef's knife. (Some squashes may need to be cooked whole.) Scoop out the seeds and fibers. If peeled chunks are required, cut the squash into pieces, then peel the pieces with a sharp paring knife. However, it is usually best to cook the squash in its shell, then puree the cooked pulp.

Winter squash can be baked, boiled, steamed, microwaved, or sautéed. To bake, cut the squash in half, place the halves cutside up in a baking pan, add $\frac{1}{2}$ inch of water, cover with foil, and bake at 400°F until tender.

To boil squash whole or in pieces, place the squash in boiling water and cook until tender. (Boiling whole is the best way to prepare spaghetti squash.) To steam, place squash chunks in the basket of a steamer and steam until tender.

*Butternut squash*

## SERVING SUGGESTIONS

Nothing is simpler than baking a halved acorn squash with butter and brown sugar or maple syrup. It also looks pretty (cut the squash crosswise to preserve the scalloped edge) and tastes delicious served with roasted chicken, turkey, lamb, or beef. Delicata squash is also delicious prepared in this manner.

Mashed winter squash combines beautifully with other ingredients, including tomatoes, green beans, potatoes, raisins, and pecans. The flavor of squash can be highlighted with spices, including cinnamon, ginger, nutmeg, allspice, or cloves. Pureed squash can be used in pies, cakes, or cookies (think pumpkin), as well as in creamed soups, soup bases, or sauces.

Spaghetti squash is delicate, but it can carry a fresh tomato sauce or a light cream sauce with grated cheese. Also try a vinaigrette dressing over cooled spaghetti squash for a dish not unlike pasta salad.

## BUTTERNUT SQUASH PIE
### Makes one 9-inch pie

1 medium-sized butternut squash (about 3 pounds)
1 teaspoon ground cinnamon
½ teaspoon ground ginger
1 teaspoon salt
½ cup pure maple syrup
½ cup honey
5 eggs, lightly beaten
¾ cup heavy cream
1 9-inch ready-to-bake pie crust

Preheat the oven to 450°F. Using a large chef's knife, halve the squash lengthwise, scoop out the seeds and fibers, and bake or steam until tender. After the squash has cooled, scrape the flesh from the skin and place it in a blender or the bowl of a food processor, and puree. Transfer the puree to a large mixing bowl.

Add the spices, salt, syrup, and honey and mix. Fold the eggs into the mixture, then slowly add the cream and mix well.

Pour the mixture into the pie crust. Bake the pie for 10 minutes; reduce the temperature to 350°F and bake for another 45 minutes, or until the filling is set. Serve warm or cold.

# WOOL & SHEEPSKIN

Until the mid-nineteenth century, New York State was America's primary sheep-producing region. With the settlement of the west, sheep farming grew to be big business, eclipsing the small Hudson Valley sheep farms. Nevertheless, more than 150 shepherds still work in this region, tending herds that range from a few pets to several hundred sheep.

Raising sheep for meat is the most lucrative aspect of the business. In recent years, thanks to a change in law, sheep can now be bred in the United States to produce milk and other dairy products. Of course, sheep are also bred for wool and sheepskin, and these products are sold by Greenmarket shepherds.

## WOOL

Sheep are sheared only once a year, each one producing from 8 to 20 pounds of wool. After shearing, the wool is "scoured," or cleaned, then goes to mills in Vermont and Canada for spinning. At Greenmarket, shepherds are permitted to have their wool processed off-farm as long as they receive their own animals' wool back from the processor.

Wool yarn available at Greenmarket comes in natural colors ranging from pure white to deep brown, as well as in dyed colors, from both natural dyes and synthetic dyes. Some home-crafted products are also sold (the items must be made by the farmers from their own animals' wool), including mittens, scarves, caps, and sweaters.

## SHEEPSKIN

Lovely sheepskin (both fleece and untooled leather) is sold by shepherds. In some cases, these are tooled into rugs, mittens, hats, slippers, and gloves.

W S S F

## MARGRIT & ALBRECHT PICHLER

MOREHOUSE FARM • Dutchess County • Red Hook, New York 12571
Stands at Union Square (Manhattan); and Grand Army Plaza (Brooklyn)

The enchanting 200-year-old Morehouse farmhouse sits close to the road, offering a sense of warmth and friendliness. Incongruously, an extraordinary flock of peacocks patrols the lawn, a proprietary dog guards the driveway, and several cats rush to greet visitors. Most important, more than 600 bleating sheep, housed in several small barns across the property, let you know that this is most definitely a sheep farm.

Morehouse Farm is the home of Margrit Lohrer Pichler, a graphic designer, and her husband, Albrecht, an architect. In 1985, when the Pichlers decided to raise sheep, they immediately turned to the production of wool (as opposed to meat), given their artistic bents and the fact that Margrit is a crackerjack knitter. Once they decided to produce wool, they soon realized they had no choice but to raise merino sheep, which for centuries have produced the finest wool in the world. (Black merino wool is more rare than cashmere.)

The popularity of merino sheep has ebbed and flowed over the centuries. Only 50 years ago, merinos were the most popular sheep in the United States, but by the 1970s they were designated as rare. The Pichlers have worked hard to repopularize the breed. When they began farming, their goal was to be the most important merino breeders in North America—and they have succeeded.

Today, the Pichlers' wool is sold to stores throughout the country and to famous designers like Ralph Lauren. They have a retail shop at the farm where they sell one-of-a-kind sweaters, mittens, hats, knitting kits, and other products, which are designed and knitted by Margrit. Although Greenmarket is not the biggest part of their business, being part of it helps Margrit and Albrecht stay in touch with consumers. Devoted knitters have become like family to them, coming back every week to show them their progress.

# ZUCCHINI & SUMMER SQUASH

*Zucchini squash*

Summer squash and zucchini, together with the wide range of winter squashes, belong to the gourd family. Although we associate these squashes with Italy and France, they were originally native to North America, and, together with corn and beans, served as the basis for the cuisines of North American and South American Indians.

## VARIETIES

**SUMMER SQUASHES.** These squashes are divided into several horticultural groups going by such common names as scalloped (or pattypan), straightneck, or crookneck, which tend to identify their shapes. They come in a variety of colors: bright yellow, many shades of green, and white, with and without striations. All have a mild, delicate flavor.

**ZUCCHINI.** Zucchini is a specific variety of summer squash. It is cylindrical, pale to dark green in color, with pale striations and mottling. The flesh is a pale cream color with a light, fresh flavor. Zucchini tends to be a bit less watery than its summer squash cousins. Although it was originally native to North America, zucchini is considered to be one of the great treasures of Italian cuisine.

## SELECTING

Choose small squashes, the smaller the better, usually no more than 5 or 6 inches in length and no broader than 2 inches in diameter for crookneck squash and zucchini, or less than 5 or 6 inches in diameter for round and pattypan squashes. For stuffed squash, you can select larger vegetables, but the dish will be more flavorful if made with several smaller ones. Look for a bright color and a glossy skin; the squash should feel firm and crisp, not limp.

## Storing

Store unwashed summer squash in a plastic bag in the vegetable crisper of the refrigerator for no more than five days.

## Putting Up

Freezing or canning summer squash or zucchini is tricky, as this process may reduce the squash to mush. Both summer squash and zucchini can be pickled. Making a squash puree and freezing it is the best preserving method; frozen puree will last for a year.

## Preparing

Summer squash and zucchini have very tender skin, so, with the exception of removing blemishes gently with a vegetable peeler, you need not peel the squash before cooking or serving raw. Just before cooking, soak the squash in cool water for about ten minutes, then rinse thoroughly in cold water to remove soil.

## Serving Suggestions

Summer squash can be prepared in myriad ways. Gently steamed or sautéed, it makes an ideal accompaniment to any poultry, fish, or meat dish. Yellow and crookneck squash are wonderful pureed in a cream soup. Sliced summer squash makes a marvelous addition to soups and stews, and is equally delectable served raw in salads or crudité platters. Larger squashes are delicious stuffed with meat, chicken, vegetable, rice, kasha, or barley.

Young zucchini takes on the flavors of garlic, basil, oregano, marjoram, curry, and other pungent herbs and spices extremely well. It is delicious fried in batter, deep fried, or sautéed to serve as a side dish or over pasta. Because of its naturally sweet flavor, zucchini also adds an interesting note to baked goods, such as bread and pancakes.

*Various summer squashes*

# AUTHOR'S THANKS

Putting together a book like this one is like baking bread. You can mix up the basic dough fairly easily, but complicated processes like kneading and rising must occur before you can enjoy the final loaf. I am grateful to many people for helping me with the hard parts.

First, very special thanks to Barry Benepe. Barry let me tag along with him as he checked markets, answered endless questions over many months, and played a major role in developing the Harvest Chart that appears here. I thank him for all his help on this book, but even more, for creating Greenmarket in the first place.

Special thanks, too, to Barry's co-founders, Lys McLaughlin and Bob Lewis. Lys spent hours explaining the intricacies of "the mayor's office" to me, then helped to edit the short history of Greenmarket that appears here. Bob graciously took the time to explain the politics of regional markets, and the joys of starting one. Both Lys and Bob are very special people.

I am grateful to several others at Greenmarket, especially Tony Mannetta, Tom Strumolo, and Lyn Peemueller. Two other Greenmarket devotees, Danny Meyer and Peter Hoffman, also gave generously of their time and insights, and I thank them.

I am grateful to all 200 Greenmarket farmers, and especially thank the following for agreeing to be interviewed: Allison Appleby, Stewart Borowsky, Frank and Ann Bulich, Tom and Nancy Clark, Pam Clarke, Judy Clarke, Pam Cohen, Joan D'Attolico, Sue D'Attolico, and especially Vince D'Attolico, Tanya Dirago, John Gorzynski, Joe Greblocki, Tom Halik, Bernadette and Walter Kowalski, Beth Linskey, Bob and Alice Messerich, Clarence Martin, John Martini, Ken Migliorelli, Alfred Milanese, Cathy, Ronny, Sid, Rick (and Marsha, Emma, and Lucy) Osofsky, Alex Paffenroth, Dorothy Pitts, Carmela Quattrociocchi, Margrit Pichler, Joel Podkaminer, Elizabeth Ryan, Tim and Jill Stark, Fred Wilklow, and David Yen.

The beauty of this book is due, in large part, to the skills of photographer Andrea Sperling. Beyond appreciating Andrea's professionalism, I thank her for always remaining optimistic and unflappable. I also thank Grace Sperling for waiting to make her appearance until after her mom had finished shooting, and Shawn Brewer for introducing Andrea to me in the first place.

This book would not be complete without delicious recipes. I am grateful to all the people listed on page 254 for permitting their recipes to be used, and I offer special thanks to Narcisse Chamberlain, Rachel Ginsberg, John Hadamuscin, Terrie Mangrum, Alfred Milanese, Andrea Sperling, Lars White, Eileen Yin-fei Lo, and Grace Young for their particular generosity.

I worked with a terrific team at Stewart, Tabori & Chang. Michelle Sidrane, the former CEO, brought the book in; publisher Leslie Stoker, with a fine eye and infinite patience, watched over it; and Leslie's assistant, Julie Ho, remained always helpful. I thank them all. Thanks, too, to Deirdre Duggan for shepherding this complicated project through the production process, and to Michael Gray and Jack Lamplough for their much appreciated enthusiasm.

The design and the management of editorial processes was handled by Beth Tondreau and her fantastic staff at BTD. With characteristic grace and professionalism, Beth Tondreau created the book's beautiful and utterly appropriate design. With flexibility, skill, and good humor, Kim Johnston, Dan Rodney, and Niccole White handled the myriad editorial and artistic details. The book was beautifully edited by Barbara Machtiger and Ann ffolliott, and I thank them heartily.

Helene Silver of City & Company came up with the idea for this book, and I thank her for planting the seeds.

Many years ago, Narcisse Chamberlain taught me much of what I know about editing cookbooks. I have dedicated this book to her, and I hope she finds that I took her valuable lessons to heart.

# Index

# METRIC CONVERSIONS

## WEIGHT EQUIVALENTS

*The metric weights given in this chart are not exact equivalents, but have been rounded up or down slightly to make measuring easier.*

| AVOIRDUPOIS | METRIC |
|---|---|
| ¼ oz | 7 g |
| ½ oz | 15 g |
| 1 oz | 30 g |
| 2 oz | 60 g |
| 3 oz | 90 g |
| 4 oz | 115 g |
| 5 oz | 150 g |
| 6 oz | 175 g |
| 7 oz | 200 g |
| 8 oz (½ lb) | 225 g |
| 9 oz | 250 g |
| 10 oz | 300 g |
| 11 oz | 325 g |
| 12 oz | 350 g |
| 13 oz | 375 g |
| 14 oz | 400 g |
| 15 oz | 425 g |
| 16 oz (1 lb) | 450 g |
| 1½ lb | 750 g |
| 2 lb | 900 g |
| 2¼ lb | 1 kg |
| 3 lb | 1.4 kg |
| 4 lb | 1.8 kg |

## VOLUME EQUIVALENTS

*These are not exact equivalents for American cups and spoons, but have been rounded up or down slightly to make measuring easier.*

| AMERICAN | METRIC | IMPERIAL |
|---|---|---|
| ¼ t | 1.2 ml | |
| ½ t | 2.5 ml | |
| 1 t | 5.0 ml | |
| ½ T (1.5 t) | 7.5 ml | |
| 1 T (3 t) | 15 ml | |
| ¼ cup (4T) | 60 ml | 2 fl oz |
| ⅓ cup (5T) | 75 ml | 2½ fl oz |
| ½ cup (8T) | 125 ml | 4 fl oz |
| ⅔ cup (10T) | 150 ml | 5 fl oz |
| ¾ cup (12 T) | 175 ml | 6 fl oz |
| 1 cup (16 T) | 250 ml | 8 fl oz |
| 1¼ cups | 300 ml | 10 fl oz (½ pt) |
| 1½ cups | 350 ml | 12 fl oz |
| 2 cups (1 pint) | 500 ml | 16 fl oz |
| 2½ cups | 625 ml | 20 fl oz (1 pint) |
| 1 quart | 1 litre | 32 fl oz |

## OVEN TEMPERATURE EQUIVALENTS

| OVEN | °F | °C | GAS MARK |
|---|---|---|---|
| Very cool | 250-275 | 130-140 | ½ - 1 |
| Cool | 300 | 150 | 2 |
| Warm | 325 | 170 | 3 |
| Moderate | 350 | 180 | 4 |
| Moderately hot | 375 | 190 | 5 |
| | 400 | 200 | 6 |
| Hot | 425 | 220 | 7 |
| | 450 | 230 | 8 |
| Very hot | 475 | 250 | 9 |